SIREN'S DANCE

SIREN'S DANCE

MY MARRIAGE TO A BORDERLINE

a case study

ANTHONY WALKER, M.D.

RODALE

Printed in the United States of America

Rodale Inc. makes every effort to use acid-free ∞ , recycled paper ♻ .

Book design by Joanna Williams

Cover photograph © by Bilderberh/Photonica

Diagnostic criteria for Borderline Personality Disorder on pages 172–174 comes from *Diagnostic and Statistical Manual of Mental Disorders*, Fourth Edition, Washington, D.C., American Psychiatric Association, 1994. Used with permission.

Library of Congress Cataloging-in-Publication Data

Walker, Anthony.
    Siren's dance : my marriage to a borderline : a case study / Anthony Walker.
        p.   cm.
    ISBN 1–57954–831–8 hardcover
    1. Walker, Anthony—Marriage—Biography.   2. Sacks, Michelle—Mental health—Biography.   3. Borderline personality disorder—Patients—United States—Biography.   I. Title.
RC569.5.B67W35   2003
362.1'9685852'0092—dc21   2003007884

Distributed to the book trade by St. Martin's Press

2 4 6 8 10 9 7 5 3 1   hardcover

Visit us on the Web at www.rodalestore.com, or call us toll-free at (800) 848-4735.

WE **INSPIRE** AND **ENABLE** PEOPLE TO IMPROVE
THEIR LIVES AND THE WORLD AROUND THEM

FOREWORD

The author's personal account of his involvement with someone having borderline personality disorder is lurid, frightening, fascinating, and compelling. [Names and places have been changed, as have certain minor other details, to protect the privacy of those involved.—Ed.] This sexually and emotionally frank account realistically captures the characteristically intense appeals and disillusionments that can be expected in a relationship with someone who has the condition. The author's training as a medical doctor and psychiatrist uniquely qualifies him to balance the highly emotional recounting of his experiences with the clinically detailed record of events and circumstances. The remarkable capacity of the borderline—in this case, the author's former wife, Michelle—to transform apparent self-confidence, charm, and promise into helplessness, rage, or suicidal urges is vividly brought to life. It is clear that the author had the perspective necessary to write this lucid account only many years later, after first having gained the needed distance and perspective to enable him to recommit himself to his work, refind his bearings, and launch a new life.

But what of Michelle's family? Though the author recognizes that her parents had the same sense of unwanted responsibility as he had, he poignantly notes that they did not have the option of leaving. He, as a husband, together with the parents had offered a "holding environment" that was helpful to Michelle. Still, it was hard for him not to hold them responsible for causing Michelle's problems. The sorry truth is that with respect to borderline personality disorder, there are rarely villains. Borderline personality disorder probably doesn't come into full bloom without the nourishment provided by families, but the potential to become borderline is inborn, and the nourishment provided by families is almost always unwitting. It's just that the world of someone with borderline personality disorder is always filled with heroes and villains, and if you're not one, you're the other.

This book is an important statement that will enhance public consciousness about a disorder that is universally recognized and widely discussed within mental health circles. [See Appendix One.] Borderline personality disorder has levels of prevalence, social dysfunction, health care utilization, and chronicity that make its public-health significance similar to that of other major psychiatric disorders such as schizophrenia, bipolar disorder, or major depression, yet it has not received comparable attention. Why is this? The answer can be found in this book. Borderline personality disorder often leaves those who become intimately involved feeling guilty, helpless, and like they have personally failed. This is most true for family members or spouses, but it is also true for clinicians. These are hardly the experiences that people want to "go public" with.

As much as I embrace the hope that this book will increase

public consciousness about a neglected psychiatric disorder, I also have hope that it will find a place within the training of mental health clinicians. Such trainees are typically overworked, but this book will certainly keep their attention. Alongside the movie *Fatal Attraction*, the book and movie *Girl, Interrupted*, and the psycho-biographical accounts of the borderline personality traits found in Princess Diana and Marilyn Monroe, this book can titillate even as it teaches. Among its take-home messages for clinicians is the value, if not the necessity, of working with others in order to keep one's perspective. Even more important is the message that the borderline patient's significant others—notably parents or spouse—experience the same dilemmas as clinicians without having the same sources of support. They need to be recruited as allies in treatment, just as this book's author has become.

—John G. Gunderson, M.D.
McLean Hospital

PREFACE

On reading a draft of the manuscript, a very dear friend of mine remarked as to how unrelenting the book was. She said that she felt despair as the story progressed, and wondered if I couldn't describe what else had happened besides my intense and pathological relationship with Michelle. I thought about this for a while and realized that I couldn't come up with any such anecdotes. The truth is that this relationship permeated every aspect of my being and my experience. I made every choice in the context of what Michelle would think and feel and how she would act or react. I couldn't ever totally relax, not until the very end. The relationship was unrelenting in its demands on me. It is hard to write that without it sounding self-piteous, but that's what it was.

I have a few thank-yous. First to Bill Malamud, a kind and thoughtful psychiatrist and supervisor, who offered me the title for the book. Then to my family, who stuck with me throughout the ordeal. To Tim, Aaron, Jan, Angelo, Hans, Howard, Gary, Jerry, and Charmaine, for still being there at the end. To Penny and Alice, who found each misplaced comma.

To Warren, who introduced me to Lou Cinquino at Rodale; to Lou, who saw the potential in the book; and to Chris Potash, who edited the text so wisely. But I could never have done this without Lauren. More than anyone, she first helped me heal, and then patiently and objectively read every word many times until it made some kind of sense.

And ultimately to Dr. John Gunderson, who gave me the final encouraging push.

SIREN'S DANCE

one

THURSDAY, FEBRUARY 7, 1985
MIAMI MEDICAL CENTER
MIAMI, FLORIDA

I was late to rounds. Already the group had moved on from the first patient, so I snuck in quietly with the other students at the back of the group. In the pecking order of medical school, we stood behind the interns, who stood behind the residents, who stood behind the professor. My cover was secure.

We congregated outside a private room as the senior resident presented the next case. "Michelle Sacks is a twenty-two-year-old single white female who was admitted to the medical ward from the emergency room last night where she had presented in an unconscious state after she overdosed on amitriptyline."

I pulled out my pocket drug-reference book and discovered that amitriptyline was in a class of antidepressant medications that led to serious heart complications and even death when a patient overdoses.

"First we pumped her stomach, and then we gave her charcoal." The charcoal absorbed any of the remaining drug in her gut, according to my book.

"Although the blood level of amitriptyline was above the

3

normal range, we monitored her heart rate and rhythm through the night and she appears to be doing well," continued the resident.

The crowd moved on to the next patient, giving me an opportunity to have a closer look at our suicide attempt. Her lips were still black from the charcoal that she had been made to drink. Her nose was bent and swollen from the pull of the nasogastric tube, which led to a bag hanging by the side of her bed and contained the former contents of her stomach. Not a pretty sight.

"Mr. Walker, can you give us a differential diagnosis for an elderly man with an enlarged liver . . . ?"

But my thoughts were stuck on the young woman. Why would anyone so young want to take her life?

Our work on the unit took the rest of the morning, and the afternoon was filled with lectures. Later that day the senior resident caught up with me. "You're interested in psych, aren't you? I want you to present a case on Monday. The chief of psychiatry is doing rounds on Monday, so I want you to pick a case with a psychiatric component."

"I'm going to interview that amitriptyline overdose," I told my classmate, Howard, later that day.

"She's cute," he laughed, "but remember, she's one of ours, you know, the Chosen People!"

Howard was my sidekick and mentor that year, our final one of medical school. An Orthodox Jew, he refused to let me drive him to the hospital on Saturdays for morning rounds. I would wind up following him in my car as he walked briskly up the road leading to the medical school, all the time arguing action versus intention. "Just get in the car," I would insist, "it's not out of my way!" But he would persist in his walking, telling me that he didn't expect a *shegetz* like me to understand.

Howard and I hardly ever talked medicine; instead we spent hours exploring human behavior and debating people's motives all the while fascinated by how, why, and what people think. Like me, he had decided to go to medical school in order to study psychiatry. I wanted to work with children and he wanted to help adults, and together we planned to fix mankind's problems.

"You know, Howard, I'm going to specialize in child psychiatry. I'll find a way to cure kids of all their worries. That way you won't have a job when I'm done," I would tease him.

"After they're finished with you, they'll all need my help," would be his retort.

The next morning I was early to rounds, but that did not change the hierarchy, and I stood at the back of the group. When we got to her bed, I peered over Howard's shoulder to get a closer look. Later she would tell me that she had noticed me staring. "God, with your big nose and curly orange hair, I thought, 'Oy, a nice Jewish boy.'" The nose is Roman, from Spanish ancestry. The curly orange hair was the unfortunate consequence of having used my housemate's shampoo. She had added a large quantity of peroxide to it to maintain her blonde hair.

After rounds, I stopped back in Michelle's room. The tubes and cables and monitors had been removed. Her dark hair was pulled back tight. Her large brown eyes filled a pretty face. Thin, manicured eyebrows and high cheekbones framed her eyes. Soft cheeks tapered down to a dimpled chin.

And then she smiled. It was a smile that stopped me from thinking. It stopped me from the purpose of my visit and instead left me gawking. Her face seemed so familiar, like that of a friend, but I couldn't place her. I continued to stare, and then it came to me like a strike: She was Vivien Leigh playing Scarlett O'Hara in *Gone with the Wind*.

I fell in love with Michelle the moment she smiled. It was as simple as that.

"My name is Anthony. I am a final-year medical student. I'd like to know more about you—I mean, talk to you so that I can present your case on Monday morning to the professor."

She continued to smile, her head half-cocked, as I struggled through my attempt to take a history.

"What is your name?" "How old are you?" "Where do you live?" "What brought you in to the hospital?" "I have to leave now. Maybe I can come back and finish tomorrow?"

"Sure," she smiled. Her smile was her lure; I was instantly seduced by it.

The dance had begun.

two

I did not sleep well. In my dreams I saw Scarlett O'Hara telling Ashley Wilkes, again and again, that she loves him, but then slapping him and proclaiming that she will hate him until she dies. Finding it hard to settle into a suddenly uncomfortable bed, I woke frequently only to be disappointed by the slow progress of the bedside clock. I was anxious to get back to the hospital. My thoughts were filled with all the questions I would ask her, filled with her beauty, filled with wanting to know her. I finally got up at 5:30.

With the end of six years of medical school only three months away, the parties heralding graduation had begun. My friends and colleagues were preparing for these as much as they were preparing for final exams, but I had some important business to attend to. I grabbed my white coat, stuffed a bagel in my mouth, and headed off. The nurses were surprised to see me on the ward.

"It's your day off! What are you doing here? Are you going to the party tonight?"

"I have to present a case on Monday. I came in to prepare."

I went into Michelle's room and found her sitting comfortably on her bed. Next to her lay a large box of what had once been Godiva chocolates but now mainly contained opened wrappers. She smiled, but this time I was prepared. "Good morning!"

She found a round chocolate and placed it slowly in her mouth, then seductively licked the tips of her fingers. "So, where do we start?" she asked.

At medical school we are taught exactly what questions to ask. Although this is important, I was finding that it was not so much the questions themselves but how well I connected with people that allowed them to tell their own unique and private stories. A large part of it was waiting and listening patiently. To understand what had driven Michelle to the depths of despair, I would need to know her more intimately than anybody I had ever interviewed before. This was not a case of cigarette smoking causing lung cancer or a skiing accident leading to a broken leg. Nothing was obvious.

"What brought you to the hospital?" I asked, sitting down on her bed.

"I took an overdose of pills."

"Can you tell me what happened?" I sat forward.

"I've been dating this guy, you see. He is rich, wonderful, and Jewish. Two months ago I found out that I was pregnant. Neither of us wanted the baby so I had an abortion. After that he stopped spending time with me. All he wanted to do was spend time with his friends, going to clubs and bars. He told me that it was too intense, that I was suffocating him. He told me that he needed space."

"Go on."

"I can't stand being alone. Men have always left me. They

8

fall in love with me and then they leave me. Obviously I'm not good enough."

"What happened next?"

"I left his house and went home. When I got there, I took a big piece of very delicious chocolate cake—you can see I love chocolate—and I swallowed a whole bottle of my mother's pills, and then I went to bed."

"How did they find you?"

"My mother called the house and the cleaning lady answered. My mother told the maid that she had something to tell me. The lady told her that she couldn't wake me up. I guess she called 911."

"Did you think you would die?"

"I did then. I was pissed when I woke up in the hospital. It's so embarrassing, but I feel so good now, so good to be alive. I'm glad that I didn't die. But you know, this morning his mother called me and told me that I was a nice girl but that I couldn't see her son anymore and that I was not to try to contact him again. He's so fucking weak. He sends his mother to do his business. What guy does that? He's so insignificant. What did I ever see in him?"

She turned to look out of the hospital window, then bowed her head and started to cry softly. I gave her a box of tissues and took her hand.

"It's going to be all right," I said, squeezing her hand. "Here, have another chocolate." She smiled.

I continued the interview. She told me she was the oldest of three children. She had gone to an art college, and she loved to paint flowers. She said she would take a large canvas and draw bubbles upon bubbles of color in oil using big strokes

9

until the whole thing fused into a field of flowers. One brother was a junior in college, majoring in math and economics. He had a predilection for hanging out at casinos playing poker and coming home at all hours, but he made money at it so her parents did not care. The youngest was quiet and a senior in high school.

Her parents were well-to-do and had a grand home in Coral Gables, a leafy suburb of Miami. She told me that her mother bullied her father. Her mother was Jewish and her father a Cuban atheist who refused to speak Spanish—"the language of that bastard Castro," he had asserted. He had even given up his surname, Sanchez, and taken his wife's last name, as further protest against "what that Communist is doing to Cuba." Despite his lack of faith, the family celebrated both Christian and Jewish holidays. For her mother, the more holidays there were, the better. She ran a cooking school and catering service that boomed during the holidays. "My dad doesn't confront my mother. He goes along with everything she says, but he can have a temper."

She loved her grandmother. "She has unconditional love for me, even when I need some extra money," laughed Michelle. "She's a real character. One day the telephone company came to her apartment saying that they had to fix her phone. She told them that it couldn't be because her phone wasn't broken, but that maybe it was the next-door phone. They knocked next door but the little old lady was out. She told them that they could use her balcony to get into the next-door apartment. Well, to cut a long story short, they went in through the balcony, robbed the neighbor, and went out her front door. She even offered them a drink for the fine service that they were

10

providing, and for their inconvenience. But when her neighbor came home, oy, she never heard the last of it."

I still did not have a sense of why she had wanted to kill herself. She was so young, so vibrant, and so beautiful. My textbook taught that it was single, alcoholic, older men who were most at risk for committing suicide. She had told me that her life was not worth living after her boyfriend had left her. Why would anybody want to leave her? And even so, what could be so painful about being left that only death could relieve? I asked her more questions but had trouble focusing on her answers. She intrigued me in a way that I had never felt before. I felt myself staring at her face, examining it for some possible imperfection, but there was none.

Finally I said, "I have no more questions. Thank you. Do you have any questions for me?"

"Yes. How old are you?"

"Twenty-five. Why do you ask?"

"You are so young. You're the best doctor in the whole hospital," she laughed.

"Final-year student," I corrected her as I floated out of the room. "I'll see you Monday."

three

The presentation was a disaster. The conference room was filled with thirty or more doctors and medical students who were at various stages of training, along with their professors of medicine and psychiatry who presided over the proceedings. Having concentrated only on the psychological aspects of the case, and on suicide in general, I hadn't prepared any of the clinical material. I couldn't remember the treatment of depression or the genetics of mental illness. My mind was not on the work. I felt embarrassed that I could not answer some of the more important aspects of tricyclic antidepressant overdose. The chief of psychiatry saved the day by talking about the diagnosis and treatment of depression.

Despite the failure of my presentation, it was precisely because of my intrigue with the mind gone awry that I had gone to medical school. I wanted to study medicine to become a psychiatrist. I was fascinated that the most complex organ of all, the brain, often suffered the most, and yet there was nothing visibly broken that people could point to and understand. No one ever said, "Did you hear that Johnny had an accident and now he is serotonin-deficient and he is going to have to wear a cast on his head for the rest of his life?" It seemed that psychological pain was the least visible of all and the easiest to blame on the sufferer.

Afterward, the chief of psychiatry pulled me aside. "Anthony, be careful. The nurses told me that you came in Saturday morning and spent quite a few hours with her, but you didn't prepare for the discussion. She is lovely, but it is more complicated than you can imagine. Don't get involved. She suffers from borderline personality disorder. Read about it. She is very ill. I can see that you want to help her, but it is a very destructive disorder. She told you herself that men always end up leaving her. It is so easy to miss because borderlines can be so charming and manipulative. She will need more and more from you, but you will never be able to give enough. Her need is unquenchable. She will suck you dry and destroy your spirit."

I did not believe him. He was wrong. What Michelle needed was love. No one could charm and manipulate me. Anyway, he had warned me, so I would be on the lookout for manipulation. In any case, who wasn't manipulative?

Later, over coffee, I looked for some support from Howard. "We are all manipulative, aren't we? I mean, a child learns that when he cries his mother comes to feed him. Eventually the mother realizes what's going on, so she lets him cry until he stops and then feeds him. So he learns to stop crying and manipulates her again. The professor speaks of manipulation as if it's a bad thing."

Howard thought about this for a while then said, "It *is* a bad thing when you use blackmail, like the threat of an emotional outburst, to get your way or when you intentionally pick on someone's weakness to get your way."

I did not worry about manipulation. I was sad because

13

Michelle was going to be discharged in the afternoon, and I wanted to know more about her. I still didn't understand exactly why she had wanted to die. Did she have no dreams for the future? I wanted to know what it would feel like to hug her and tell her that I was certain that everything would work out well for her. I remembered a first-year medical school seminar that warned us against becoming too familiar or too close with our patients. I had shaken many of my patients' hands, and had put my arm around an older patient's shoulders as he faced chemotherapy, but never before had the prospect of physical contact with someone I had worked with felt confusing. How would that ethics class have dealt with this situation? I was sure it would never have been approved, so reluctantly I decided against the hug.

But I did visit Michelle in her room once more before her discharge.

"Good-bye."

"Good-bye," she said, offering her hand. I held it in mine, wondering how I could extend the time with her, but I had no ideas. At least I was happy that she looked as well as she did so soon after having made such a serious suicide attempt.

"Good luck. I'm sure that you'll be okay." And with that I walked out of her room and, I thought, out of her life.

I went looking for Howard and found him in the laboratory, laboring with the viewfinder of a microscope as he examined a patient's sputum. I told him that Michelle had gone. "You know, her fall into hopelessness and her recovery, her intense soul-searching, and her playfulness validate my belief that there are still wild, beautiful, emotionally intense women out there. Isn't it a wonderful world?"

Howard was relieved. "I'm glad that she's gone, for your sake. You don't know what you were getting involved with. Rescue fantasy is the classic pitfall of the novice therapist. I brought you this paper I found in the *American Journal of Psychoanalysis* that talks about it."

The article dealt with the finding that many inexperienced therapists feel that they can cure borderline patients simply by trying as hard as they can and by caring enough. They initially intrude into all aspects of the patient's life, causing the patient to increasingly depend on the therapist. For the therapist, there is great narcissistic appeal in being so needed, but there is also great disappointment, as the work results in little change. Over time the therapist burns out, gradually growing to resent and blame the patient. Finally the therapist can no longer meet what he feels to be the unrealistic demands of the patient and terminates therapy. In the end the patient is hurt even further by this abandonment.

What a mess, I thought to myself. Maybe it was true what some people say, that you had to be crazy to be a psychiatrist.

Howard's paper was interesting, but I failed to see what it had to do with me. It dealt concretely with patients and therapists. I had no intention of becoming Michelle's therapist. I just wanted her to feel self-worth. I wanted to tell her that her life was not meaningless, that she had talents and grace, that she was funny and cute. Also I had no sense that I had a need to rescue her. She so quickly appeared to have recovered that there didn't seem to be anything from which to rescue her. I reassured Howard that I could take care of myself.

That evening I went to the school library. Howard had recommended a book by a Dr. John Gunderson. "The guy is from

McLean Hospital in Boston. It's the most famous psychiatric hospital in the world. He wrote a whole book on borderline personality."

In six years of medical school we had spent only two weeks in the psychiatry wards. During that time we learned about depression, mania, and schizophrenia. That experience, and ten classroom lectures on psychiatry, was the extent of our exposure to the complicated field of disrupted brain functioning and disturbed behavior. No one had mentioned personality disorders, so I had no reason to consider them important. I believed that everyone had his or her own personality, an individual style. Some people were more difficult to deal with than others, but I didn't think that meant they had a "disorder."

When I found the Gunderson book, entitled *Borderline Personality Disorder*, published in 1984, I noticed that it had been checked out only a handful of times. This reassured me that not too many others seemed to worry about the condition. I read the chapter that described the criteria necessary to make the diagnosis of borderline personality disorder, or BPD, but other than the suicide attempt, Michelle didn't seem to meet any of them. What struck me more than anything else was that she had been in such great spirits when she left the hospital after a short stay. The patients I had seen in the psychiatry wards remained there for weeks or months at a time and often seemed depressed. Michelle didn't look like someone who had a long-term, severe psychiatric condition. Of course, in reality I had known her only for the five days she had spent in the hospital; but still, she had shared so much of herself and so many of her life experiences with me, and in such a lucid manner. Surely this was not the face of severe mental illness.

I continued to read through Dr. Gunderson's book, even though the language seemed technical to me:

Although the concept of a transitional object seems more compatible with the observations on the dependency and separation sensitivity of Borderline patients than does the concept of a self-object, the distinction between these two concepts is murky.

What was a "transitional object"? What was "separation sensitivity"? How did these terms apply to Michelle? The symptoms seemed so much more complicated than how she had presented. I doubted that she really had the disorder.

four

One day when I was nine years old, our family went to the beach. A fisherman was casting his lines off the rocks nearby. I took my plastic pail and went to sit by him. Over the next hour his catch was plentiful, but many fish were too small for his basket. He took them off the hook and threw them aside. Occasionally a brave gull would venture close to pick the easy meal. It saddened me that the fish might be suffering, so I filled my bucket with water and put the discarded fish into it before the gulls or dry land could do them further damage. Soon I had five fish and, as the fisherman was done for the day, I headed back to my family.

Once home, the fish did not appear to be all that happy as they swam sluggishly in the warm, murky water. We had a small plastic yard pool that we barely used but looked to be the right size for my fish. I filled the pool with fresh water and then dumped my bucket into it. Immediately the fish seemed to be in trouble. I hurried to tell my father, who explained that the fish would die because they were saltwater fish and couldn't live in fresh water. I ran to the kitchen for the salt shaker, then headed back to the pool and dumped the entire contents into the water. "Come on, fish, live. Come on, fish," I pleaded, but to no avail.

Then there was the time when I was a bit older and a neighbor came over with his new pellet gun. He aimed it at a pigeon sitting on a branch of a large oak in our yard and pulled the trigger. The bird dropped to the ground and started flopping about. I picked it up and saw that it had been shot through its left eye. Distressed, I took it to my mother and begged her to take me to the veterinarian so that we could save it. The bird died en route.

"You have always cared for the very weakest, the most hopeless cases," my mother once observed. Perhaps that was why at medical school I had elected to serve an internship at a clinic in the central highlands region of rural Costa Rica. With few medical services and little education offered, prenatal care was rare in the village. One day a young mother brought her three-week-old son to the clinic. He had been listless for two days. The mother's family didn't know of the child's existence; she had been too ashamed to tell them. But now she was terrified of losing the child. She confessed that she had had a difficult time breastfeeding him. The child was terribly dehydrated, with sunken eyes and a hollow belly. We couldn't even find a vein to give him fluids. Half an hour later, the child died. That was the first time I cried at medical school. It was also the last. An intern pulled me aside. "If it gets to you that bad each time they die, you gotta rethink this profession. It's going to happen all the time."

I cried not just for the death itself, but for how terrible it must have been for the mother and the fears that had made her avoid seeking help. I cried for the loss and the guilt that she must have felt. I was angry that the system had failed this mother by not providing her with education or easy access to medical care. I promised myself that in the future I would not let my emotions affect my judgment, but I also would not lose sight of the need to take care of people.

five

THURSDAY, FEBRUARY 14

I kept thinking about Michelle. Her discharge just days earlier seemed like an eternity ago. I wondered how she was and if she was taking care of herself, but I resisted the urge to call her. And so, when the nurse manager handed me the message that Michelle's mother had called and wanted me to call back and had said it was important, my body tensed and my hands became clammy. It was the feeling of being fourteen and in love again, of waiting for the phone to ring after a first date.

"Hello, Mrs. Sacks? This is Anthony. You had called looking for me? Is everything all right?"

"Oh, hello! I just wanted to tell you that Michelle is doing much better. We wanted to thank you for everything you did."

"Really, I did nothing. You seem to have a nice family. You all pulled together when Michelle needed it most. It's that kind of love that heals."

"You don't understand. We haven't seen her this happy in a long time. Anyway, another reason I called is that a friend of ours is having a big party on Saturday. It's for their daughter, who is turning twenty-one. Michelle was wondering if you would go as her escort. It would mean so much to her if you went. She doesn't have a date since she broke up with her boyfriend."

The ethics lecturer had warned about not getting too close to our patients, but was Michelle my patient? She was no longer under my care in any way. The situation seemed less ambiguous than wondering if a hug was crossing some boundary. In any case, she was reaching out to me. "I really don't see why not. I had been wondering how Michelle was doing. I'd be happy to go."

"Good! If you could, be here by seven for pre-party drinks." She gave me the directions to her house and I told her I'd be there on time. I wondered why Michelle herself had not called. Maybe she worried that I would say no and the rejection would have been too much after everything else that had happened. That evening I set out for my usual five-mile run. I noticed that I ran a little faster than usual, and, having completed the loop, I repeated the distance.

The rest of the week sped by until Saturday, when time seemed to stop. Every minute dragged on. I read the newspaper over breakfast, took a shower, and shaved, but that took up only a half-hour or so. I went for a long run and took another shower. I watched some television, then the clock. I tried to read to distract myself but nothing helped. I could not keep Michelle out of my mind. Was it possible, as she had said, that she was so much in love with her boyfriend that breaking up was intolerable? But if so, why was she now so happy? Was it me? Had I made so much of an impression on her that our brief encounter let her believe that she could find such love again? Was I delusional to even think so?

Eventually the time passed, and as evening approached I showered for the third time that day. I carefully chose a pair of trendy olive-green jeans to wear with black patent leather shoes and a light-green-and-white-striped dress shirt. Unable to stop pacing, I left early and arrived at Michelle's with twenty minutes to spare. I drove around the block four or five times, not wanting to appear too eager. I parked the car outside the wrought-iron gates, which opened onto a long brick driveway. I blew a breath out forcibly through pursed lips, willing myself to relax, as I walked to the house. As there was no doorbell I could find, I reached for the iron knocker, which was shaped like a mermaid and had a welcoming smile. Michelle opened the door before I had a chance to knock.

She glowed. She wore a low-cut floral dress, which she told me was Gianfranco Ferré. Her hair was pulled up, to open up her face, and then fell in soft braids onto her open back. Two large gold hoops dropped from soft lobes. Her white smile was made all the brighter by the contrast with her Revlon-red lips. Finally, high heels helped to further define her well-toned and tanned legs. "Well, are you just going to stand there? Come and meet the rest of the family."

She led me to the living room, where her parents and brothers were sitting around a large glass cocktail table. Her father, dressed casually, stood up and smiled a welcoming smile while offering a handshake and a pat on the back. "Good to meet you. Can we call you Anthony?" Michelle's mother remained seated but moved to the edge of the couch, also offering her hand and insisting that I sit. "What can we get you to drink?" She seemed satisfied with herself and, like Michelle, wore a low-cut dress. Michelle's brothers showed less enthusiasm in meeting me but were polite and seemed anxious to leave for the party. Both boys were tall and handsome, and it was clear that the Sacks family was, if nothing else, good-looking. Michelle's father insisted on my joining him in a glass of wine prior to our departure, to the consternation of his sons; but I really finished the glass quickly, which met with clear approval from the boys. "Can we go now?"

The party was to be at the house of a friend, a man they called Tio, who lived in Little Havana, not far from Domino Park. I had been to the park on occasion in search of a game of chess. This, together with the ever-present cigar smoke and an emphatic point of view, was always on offer. I met an old man who called himself Abuelo and told me that he had once played against the great Capablanca. "I came very close to beating him, but he checkmated me before I could him," he proclaimed triumphantly. Even the chess was lively in the heart of Miami.

"Anthony, we are probably going to be there quite late, so you might want to take your car," suggested Michelle's mother. "Michelle, you can drive with Anthony, if you want." Her mother had it all figured out.

At the party she quickly reached for one drink, and then another. Next she had two glasses of Merlot with dinner. "I don't usually drink this much," she laughed, "but I do feel less nervous when I drink." It was clear that I wasn't going to understand anything deep about her that night. It was not going to be a night for talking, so I joined her when a Chardonnay was served. Eventually the dance music started, and after each of the first three dances she downed another glass of wine before she abruptly stopped drinking. "I can't get too drunk tonight, you know. I've got plans."

She flirted conspicuously with admiring men, yet all the

24

time stayed close to me. She reminded me of a child coyly playing peek-a-boo with strangers while holding on to her mother's leg. But there was more than just flirting and drinking. There was hip gyrating, jacket twirling, and skirt hiking. There was laughing and teasing, playful taunting and hinting. We had been at the party for just over two hours when she grabbed my hand and led me outside. The humid South Florida evening enveloped us. She pressed me back against my father's 1979 Jaguar XJ6, which he had unexpectedly loaned me for the evening.

"Tonight you got the best, and you know it. You saw the other men looking at me. You know they wanted me, but I am with you and I want you to take me home now."

I had never been on a date as unpredictable as this. I could not tell how it would end, and this uncertainty intrigued me. Michelle was in total control now. I had been expecting a somewhat subdued evening spent in reflection and talk, but there had been little of either. Instead I was being seduced by a modern-day Scarlett O'Hara, and I was not inclined to stop the seduction.

I opened the passenger door and she slid into her seat. Driving west on Calle Ocho, it was difficult to concentrate, but it was even more difficult to believe that only a week earlier, modern medicine had ensured that Michelle's suicide attempt did not succeed. A tough, self-confident sexiness had replaced vulnerability, innocence, and openness. I tuned the radio to a local music station. She sang along with a Tina Turner song, "You're simply the best . . ."

Now I would caution any friend to be careful in a relationship with a potentially suicidal woman with few inhibitions, but the rational mind flooded by libido is no longer rational. This was a strange moment for me. I felt that I had been sucked into a new version of *Gone with the Wind*. I was the protagonist. Yet I had lost sight of the fact that Hollywood movies end after two hours. Moreover, after the show you get to go home.

Michelle's parents were still carousing at the party when we arrived at her house. "My parents won't be back for a while," she teased as she opened the door with her key. Still in the dark, she offered, "You didn't have much to drink. My dad has a bottle of bubbly in the fridge. Let's toast to life!"

In the kitchen she tore open the refrigerator door and, silhouetted by the light inside, she handed me the bottle. Losing myself in the moment, I shook the champagne the way racecar drivers do after having won a race, and the cork popped easily as the white foam spewed out. I found two flutes and turned to offer her a drink. She had stripped down to her waist and held her breasts together in her cupped hands. "I want you to drink from me!" I nearly dropped the bottle. She laughed. "I want you to pour it between my breasts and drink from me. God, that will turn me on!"

The enchantment was complete, and I did as she instructed. As I poured and drank, she threw her head back and held mine to her chest. "Kiss my nipples."

Suddenly she pulled my head back. "Quick," she insisted, "come with me to the living room!" I did not hear the car approaching. She stripped completely and lay down on a plush white shag, directing me all the while with skilled hands. It was all the time I needed to reach a quick climax. She jumped up and quickly got dressed, urging me to do the same. Then she turned on the light. "Damn. Help me move this couch over the stain. I made a mess with my period. I'll clean it up tomorrow."

We then sat on the couch as her parents entered the room. I felt awkward and disheveled. I sensed the sweat forming on my brow. She sat saintly cool.

"Hi, dear. Have a nice time?"

"Yes, thanks, Mom. And Anthony took good care of me."

"Well, goodnight. Thanks for escorting Michelle." After a pause, she added, "Darling, please clean up the champagne before you go to bed. You spilled some on the floor in the kitchen."

six

I had always enjoyed living on the edge but on reflection, my edges were safe and relatively sure. Being with Michelle was different. It was dangerously exhilarating, like a joyride on a roller coaster in the dark after the park had closed for the day.

I had been brought up in a devout Catholic family, the eldest of eight children. We were born in four countries on three continents, a consequence of my father's international import-export business. I was born in Indiana; one sibling was born in England, four in Spain, and two in Kenya. I have asked my father many times why they decided to settle in Miami, and his answer changes each time.

We had moved to Miami in the late 1970s, after our time in Kenya, which had a British-style conservatism that appealed to my father. I suspect that the permissive sex-and-drugs culture of the United States in the 1960s had disgusted my parents and had motivated them to travel abroad as they did. I am not sure why they ever thought it safe to return. Maybe it was when Gerald Ford, whom my father considered to be a man of integrity, assumed the presidency. In any case, I came back to America to discover marijuana joints and *Playboy* magazine. I had a lot to experience in order to catch up to my classmates.

All this matters because in Kenya I felt I had been deprived of my chance at adolescent irresponsibility without having been given a choice. I didn't want to hear about my parents doing this for my own good. "Most people only read about what you guys have lived through," my father told us often. He was so emphatic about this particular point, I defensively reasoned, that he should like Michelle. In her he should see the perfect partner for me. My father had hungered for a diversity of experience, so wouldn't he appreciate someone as different and exotic as she was? "You learned Spanish and Swahili," my father said proudly. "None of the other guys in your class can say that." He had a point.

My mother lived by the belief that because we did not know either the time or the place of the Second Coming, any person could be the Messiah. We had to love and treat all people as if salvation itself depended upon it. Her three sisters were nuns, and there were great hopes that one of us would pursue a religious devotion.

But despite eating fish on Fridays, we laughed a lot. My mother regaled us with stories from our mischievous past. "Once I took Anthony to see my sister at the convent. While there we happened upon the Mother Superior. 'Say hello to the Mother Superior,' I told him. He was only four years old, and the Good Lord had not gifted her with looks. He said, 'Hello, Pig!' I told him to apologize immediately, and he was very ashamed and he hung his head and said, 'Sorry, Pig.'"

The four oldest children were made the guardian angels of the four youngest. Our sacred task was to protect them from all dangers, physical and spiritual. On this, too, salvation depended. Once my mother had entrusted my then-six-year-old brother, Michael, to keep my fourteen-month-old sister, Rachel, entertained in her crib while my mother went upstairs to get a blanket for her. We were in the yard and the wind had picked up. As I was the oldest child, my mother told me to keep an eye on both of my siblings. She assured us that she would be right back. We had been collecting earthworms up until that point, and we thought that showing them to my sister would entertain her. Immediately she started to cry, which Michael said meant that she was hungry. As salvation depended upon caring for our younger siblings, we fed her with the only thing at hand. Years later, *National Geographic* ran an article about a farm in Minnesota that raised earthworms for their protein content and nutritional potential. Unfortunately, we did not have that article to show in our defense when my mother returned.

My father was a practical man, which is to say that to him things needed to make sense. There was little room in his worldview for "emotionalism," as he would call it. Emotions led to a clouding of rational thought. Getting from point A to point B had to be accomplished in a straight line. If you wanted to pass a test, you studied, and if you wanted to be number one in your class, you studied hard. My mother did not care as much about tests or our being number one, as long as we were happy. My father, however, insisted that being number one would make us happy. He had little time for words not backed up by deeds. "You get your emotional makeup from your mother's side of the family," he would tell me after many of the arguments I would have with him. Still, I loved my mother's sometime-lack of rational perspective and was in awe of her intuition.

My father would be up at six in the morning and off to work but back by five to help with the homework. Each child had up to half an hour with him to review their homework. He would nurse a Scotch during the homework session, but this did not dull his determination to see that every bit of school-work had been done. Fun for him was naming the capitals of obscure countries, and it became a game that we played on Sundays during lunch. His serious manner made it a challenge for us to try to get him to ease up and laugh at silly things.

Once Michael went to a farm fair and by an outrageous stroke of luck guessed the exact number of eggs in a huge container. The first prize was a one-month-old calf. When my mother picked us up, we loaded the calf into the back of the station wagon and drove back to suburbia. We had a three-acre yard, so the calf would have plenty of grass to eat and room to roam. Moreover, we had a middle-aged sheepdog that needed company, so the calf was a hit. Initially it spent time following Rufus, the dog. The calf regarded the dog as its mother, Rufus being the only other creature that ate on all fours. But soon it ranged more freely and visited the yards and gardens of our neighbors. The calf's need for food had increased dramatically, and it was destroying large patches of yard, although it did deposit equivalent amounts of manure in return. It continued to grow and moved from soprano to tenor in a matter of weeks, mooing along with the barking dog at passing cars or pedestrians. One particularly hot summer day our bridge-playing neighbors came frantically to our house. They had left the gate to their pool open and our dog had jumped in. But of greater concern was that the young bull had followed suit and could now not get out of the pool! It left the next day for an unknown destination, a place where, my father assured us, it would be well cared for. We boycotted beef for the next two months.

I recognized the differences between my home life and that of Michelle's. Although there were many moments of fun, pranks, and outrageous adventure in our home, there was an underlying bedrock of faith and education in our home that was fundamental to the way that my parents had decided to structure our family. Michelle's family lived for the moment. Meaning came from the stimulation of the senses of smell, taste, feel, sight, and hearing. Pleasure was an end in itself. This was a new and very appealing perspective for me.

Because of this difference, I worried that my parents would see Michelle as godless and unmotivated in matters academic, hopeless enough to consider suicide, and too cute to be anything but a distraction to a young man facing medical school finals. To me she was captivating and challenging. She had pain, sorrow, and emptiness that only love and laughter would heal. She was the Messiah. My mother would understand.

I was convinced that my relationship with Michelle would move me past all the petty constraints of social expectation and rules of "acceptable" behavior. I was certain that she could teach me everything about life and pleasure that a conservative upbringing couldn't. I wanted to push our relationship further than I had ever pushed a relationship before. I was sure that it would take us to a level of emotional intensity that few people had ever experienced.

seven

LATE APRIL

For the first two months Michelle and I were inseparable. At times it felt like more than that, almost as if we had fused into one being, feeling the same feelings and thinking the same thoughts.

"I cannot stand being away from you," she would tell me. "I can't stand that you go to the hospital and care for all those other people, that you are gentle with them and worry about how they do. I can't stand that you leave me every day to go to work. I want you to be with me for always and ever. Please don't ever leave me."

"I can't stand being away from you either. I miss you just thinking about you. I'll never leave you."

One afternoon we headed from her parents' home to Tropical Park for a stroll and a talk. As evening came on, the air began to cool, and we found ourselves virtually alone. We stopped at an antique-looking bench beside a large old oak tree and sat quietly holding hands, watching the sky turn pink. Suddenly, the sprinklers turned on. Michelle jumped up in delight and skipped into the middle of the spray, drenching herself. Her wet shirt hugged her body seductively as she ran her fingers through her hair, dancing to the beat of the spurting water. I laughed and followed her. She stopped dancing and started smiling, then stared at me with the look of a cobra about to strike, all the while, yet slowly, unbuttoning her shirt. She took my hands and pulled me down to the wet grass with her. I worried that we would be seen by passersby, or worse, be arrested by the police, but none of this seemed to matter to Michelle. She kissed me, and held my hand to her breast. "Make love to me. . . ."

Pathetically, I spent little time studying for final exams. Michelle was teaching me to eat oysters with a desire seldom associated with food. She would close her eyes and tease the oyster with her tongue while holding the shell tightly in her hands, moaning softly, though never vulgarly. Her desperate need to feel was as seductive as it was intriguing. Eating was feeling, drinking was feeling, and shouting was feeling. Michelle was all about feeling deeply and genuinely. I was born again to a world where nothing was predictable and experiences were intense and memorable.

Being with Michelle was like adding a couple of dashes of Tabasco to fresh homemade vanilla ice cream. She could easily be without pleasantries. If she did not like what she considered awful food on her plate, she sent it back, with no regard for the feelings of the waiter or the chef. "This is crap; take it back. I could have made it better myself." Then seeing my surprise, she would say, "We paid for their food and for their service. We got neither. Fuck them. Next time they won't make the same mistake. If you don't demand the best, you'll never get it. We run around saying 'excuse me' and 'pardon me' when we mean 'give me the fucking service you promised!'" The honesty was so brutal and refreshing, it was hard to disagree.

eight

I began to think seriously about my future with Michelle. I had accepted an internship in Taos, New Mexico, after medical school, and I realized that if she were to join me, she would need something to keep her busy during the long hours I would be putting in. Michelle had gone to art school to hone an evident talent, but after a year-and-a-half she had left. "They really didn't have anything to teach me. I'm not interested in art history. I just want to paint." Her art was big and colorful, oils on canvas that filled beyond the frame.

"I'll paint. I'll make you a beautiful home. I'll cook for you, and I'll love you. In return, just never leave me. I have never felt such intense love from anybody I have ever been with. If you ever took it away from me, I would die."

I knew that she had had boyfriends that she had cared about in the past, and I could not see why anybody would have wanted to leave her. "What happened to your first boyfriend?"

"I was thirteen and he was so much older than me. I remember that we were on vacation with my parents. I saw him lying by the pool with his friends. I went straight up to him and told him I wanted a drink. He was twenty, but I told him I was sixteen so he wouldn't get into trouble. I had always developed quicker than my friends. I know they hated me for it. That night was my first time ever. We were together for five years, but then he joined the Air Force. He told me that he would spend every free moment with me. One day he told me to meet him at his apartment, but he was late. God, that pissed me off so much that I broke into his place. I waited and waited. I got so angry. I thought that he was with someone else, and the more I thought about it the angrier I became. I searched his whole apartment. I found a pile of old letters from his ex. I put them in the middle of his room on the rug and burnt them. It felt so good, you just don't know. How could he still keep them when he was with me? When he got back, he had some roses and chocolate for me. He found the mess, and after that he never trusted me again. He left me, like men always have. No, maybe I left him. I do that to weak men. Weak men have no balls. I need a man with balls, and you have balls."

Michelle told me repeatedly that she needed people to love her. "When I was eighteen I met a man, an actor, who instantly fell in love with me. He couldn't take his eyes off me that first night. He begged me to tour the country with him. He insisted that I would inspire him in his aspiring role as Macbeth. I agreed to go with him the next morning, and left without telling anybody. I think that my mom knew where I was, but she was happy to get rid of me for a while." She set off with the actor on his quest for significance, but the demands of auditioning and the frustrations of rejection made him moody. "Sometimes he would get pissed at not having been given the part and he would go out drinking and not come home all night. It terrified me to be left alone in an apartment in a strange city. One morning I called my mother. She wired me money and I left before he came home that night. I think that

36

he finally succeeded in acting, though. I see him on TV every so often. I could never have been with him."

"You'll do anything for love?" I asked her.

"Once I met a guy at a club. He was so nice to me and invited me back to his house. When we got there, the guy's girlfriend was in bed. He told me that it would really turn him on if I did it with his girlfriend. I liked the guy, and I had drunk too much, and she was cute. A woman's body is so much more beautiful than a man's. Sometimes it turns me on, but I only did it that once. Now I can't think of anything grosser. But I know it turns guys on when I tell them that story. You'd love to be with two women," she laughed. "But I tell you, it's not going to happen. Not with me anyway. I can't be with two people. I need one person who will love me totally and completely."

One night I sat with Michelle and her mother, sharing a sweet Australian dessert wine after dinner. Michelle excused herself from the table and her mother took advantage of her daughter's absence. "God, how I have suffered with that girl. She dropped out of college and spent every night dancing at nightclubs. One night she met a girl who was some kind of model. The girl started coming over to the house, and eventually she started spending the night at our house. She slept in Michelle's room and they would lock themselves in there. But the walls aren't that thick. I know what was going on. It went on for over two months. Then the girl would call Michelle at two and three in the morning. When I told the girl that she had to stop calling that late, Michelle freaked and broke all my chinaware. God, please don't tell her I told you. She'll go crazy."

"What happened after that?"

"The girl found herself a boyfriend and Michelle became

very depressed. We were worried and encouraged her to go out more, to start working out. She started to go to a gym and she met another woman who was just as pretty as the first. All her friends are beautiful. I think she does it because her self-esteem is so low, which I can't understand because she is more beautiful than all of them. Anyway, they soon became good friends and they decided to go on a double date. Michelle invited a man that she had been keen on. He had said that he would invite a friend, but the friend did not show. He spent his whole time talking to the other girl. Michelle said that she had to go to the powder room, but instead she came back to the house and got one of my biggest kitchen knives. She went back to the club and slashed the girl's tires. When the girl came out, Michelle chased her into the car with the knife. The wheels were destroyed as her friend tried to drive away. Anyway, we paid for the damages, but that poor girl, she must have been terrified by the way Michelle had suddenly turned on her. You know, Michelle has even threatened me with a knife. With her it's like walking on eggshells. I don't know how you do it." She shuddered as she took a sip of her wine.

Every single one of these stories seemed explainable to me in the context of rejection and disappointment in somebody who loved herself so little and who felt that she had never been unconditionally assured of love. I would change that. In any case, she had spunk; she had taken matters into her own hands, dealing with her problems in her own unconventional way. My father would never have approved. Her unpredictable self-assuredness delighted me. I was not convinced that this was the erratic behavior of a troubled mind. Perhaps she overdid it when someone crossed her, but I was not the enemy. I knew that I loved her, and she knew it too.

nine

EARLY MAY

My mother once told me that the most important lesson she could give me came from the New Testament. "Jesus once told his followers, 'My command is this: Love each other as I have loved you.' His love for us was unconditional, as must ours be for our fellow man," she told me. I was thinking of my mother's words when I drove to Michelle's house the day after my final exams.

The sun shone especially brightly that day. I changed into a pair of swimming shorts and headed for the pool. Michelle's mother came over, towel in hand, and lay down next to me.

"My husband and I have been talking. You really have become part of the family. I mean, you are almost like one of the family. Anyway, we are very worried about Michelle. She has become so attached to you. She can't stop talking about you. She cares about you a great deal. You are so good to her, and we haven't seen her this happy and relaxed and stable in a long time."

"And I am happy, too."

"Yes, but you are going to be leaving town to do your internship, and you know how she does when she is left alone."

"But she can come and visit me whenever she wants. We

talked about that already. I asked her to come with me, but I am not sure that she is ready to move away from you."

"You know that she can't deal with separation," she continued.

"Yes, but she knows that I love her. Besides, it's a separation only in space, not in heart or mind."

"Anthony, you can't build up her expectations and then take yourself away. That would be cruel, especially now that you know her as well as you do. You've seen her at her worst. Even your professor at the hospital said that she could be in a relationship but that it would have to be with a saint. You see how happy she is. You are her saint. If you left her, you would be setting us up as well. We would have to pick up the pieces yet again."

"But I am off to do my internship. I can't change that," I protested.

"Just don't leave her; it will destroy her." She left to pour herself a gin and tonic. The day had chilled a little in the afternoon sun.

Something unsettled me about the conversation with Michelle's mother. I had no thought of leaving Michelle, so what was all this about? Her words confused me. How would my leaving destroy Michelle? She had made it through life this far without me. She was an aggressive survivor, who on one occasion had taken some pills. I knew she was extreme, but I loved that in her. In the time I had been with Michelle, I had seen nothing that reflected psychotic thinking or out-of-control behavior. This validated my sense that she was destructive only when she felt betrayed. I would never betray her.

I felt that I was being manipulated. Howard had warned

me of manipulation by borderline patients, but he had said nothing about their mothers. It bothered me that she would doubt my intentions.

When I met Michelle, her beauty and her energy had enchanted me, but it was her absolute need to be loved that was most compelling. She was like a flower with some exotic pollen, and I was an intoxicated bee. It was flattering to think that this intriguing woman with such sophisticated tastes and varied life experiences could find me interesting. I could not tell a Monet from a Matisse, a flan from a crème caramel, a Versace from a Gucci. It felt good to be so wanted and needed by her; she had so much to teach me about living. This made it easy to love her and care for her. The matter of the suicide attempt was a remote memory, and one that didn't seem to fit. She made it easy for me to forget just how fragile she was.

ten

LATE MAY
MIAMI SCHOOL OF MEDICINE

Graduation night was an elegant affair. There was enough ceremony to make us believe that we had finally graduated to god-
liness. I had invited Michelle as my guest, and she sat with my
parents, sharing the moment when I could officially add an
M.D. to my name. At the end of the event, my father took me
aside, wearing a serious, nearly stern look on his face. There
were so many things in life that he took seriously that his looks
of concern held little significance to me anymore.

"Anthony, you have a whole exciting life ahead of you. I'm
worried that you are getting too involved too quickly, that you
will throw away everything you have worked for before you
even have a chance to know all your possibilities and opportunities. I am worried that you are getting so deeply involved with
someone you don't even know. I tried to talk to her. She has no
goals. She expects you to take care of her. Does she have any
idea just how busy your next year is going to be?"

I didn't want to have this discussion with him. I was sure
he would not understand how Michelle brought me the unpredictability that I wanted and needed in my life.

"Dad, don't worry. I know what I'm doing."

Michelle and I drove off to our favorite bayside café for a long talk over a long coffee. I told her about my dream of becoming a psychiatrist one day. "That's why I went to medical school. I know that the next year is going to be hell, being on call and everything. I feel so close to you, but these intense past few months that we have spent together are going to end soon. Your mother is worried that you won't be able to handle my working all the time."

"Thinking of you working so many long hours makes me sad. It makes me so sad that I miss you already and you are still here. I can't take it."

"The first year is the worst, but after that it will become easier, you'll see."

She began to cry softly and took my hands. "How do I know that it will get easier? How do I know that you won't leave me just like everybody else has?"

"Look at me. I won't leave you because I love you. I will never leave you, and you have to hold that in your heart."

She bowed her head, then softly said, "Men have always told me that they loved me and that they would never leave me, but look at me. I am still alone. You know, sometimes when you go home at night I feel that I lose you. I can't hold onto you and keep you inside me. I need to work at remembering how good you are to me."

We talked into the night. Eventually the staff asked us to leave. Michelle was still not convinced. Her experience had been one of hope followed by rejection at every turn. I wanted to show her that I meant what I was telling her. As we headed for the parking garage elevator, suddenly it hit me. I knew just what I had to say to prove to her that I loved her.

"Michelle, will you marry me?"

She stopped and looked at me, stunned.

"Do you mean that?"

"Of course I mean it. Once I finish my internship we'll get married. One year, and then we'll do it, what do you say?"

The door opened and we entered the elevator. In classic Michelle style, she kissed me so passionately and emphatically that her answer was clear.

"Let's make love right here."

"It's a glass elevator," I laughed.

"You really do love me," she said, relieved, and held my arm tight.

When we got back to her parents' house sometime after midnight, she could not wait to tell her mother. She ran excitedly down the hall to their room. The talk in the bedroom was animated, and I paced nervously back and forth in the parlor.

"He what?" I heard her mother shout out. "Is he drunk?"

"No, Mom, we haven't had anything to drink. Really, he asked me."

"Alright, dear, we'll talk about it in the morning."

Michelle returned smiling, and then hugged me. "Thank you for believing in me."

I went home with the peace of mind that Michelle could finally be certain about my sincerity. Everything would be all right now.

eleven

Michelle's mother dealt with her incredulity the way that she dealt with most other things in her life. "Let's have a party! Why don't you each invite some friends? Anthony, I'll cook a meal that will move even your dad."

Michelle's mother ran a cooking school that had been successful for more than thirty years. Her daughter's engagement party brought out the desire to flaunt her culinary skills. Immediately she got to work on the menu. First a salad of cherry tomatoes, fresh basil, chopped fresh parsley, and minced garlic on romaine lettuce dressed with a homemade mayonnaise. Freshly baked baguettes would accompany the entire meal. Following would be a whole lamb on the spit, which would be continuously basted with a marinade of oil, vinegar, mustard, garlic, salt, pepper, ginger, cumin, paprika, and rosemary. "The 1979 Arrowood Chardonnay will be in ample supply," her father had insisted, more animated than I had ever seen him.

"So will Perrier and Dom Perignon," said Michelle with a laugh. Dessert would be a chocolat poiver accompanied by a Sauterne that her father had picked out.

Amidst the preparations, I had yet to confront the hard part: telling my family, especially my father. I went for long walks and had many imaginary conversations with him. I would think of what he would say and then would argue with him. He would make a point and then I a counterpoint. Even though the conversation was imagined, I could never get him to agree with me. Still, I had to tell him. One day he came back from work in a particularly cheery mood. This would have to be the time. "Dad, I need to talk to you. . . ."

"You what?!"

"I know exactly what you think; I have gone over this conversation a thousand times in my head. But it is a matter of judgment, and I know that everything is going to come out all right."

"I have only met her three times. How can you know what I think? I don't even know what I think." He was upset and stood up from his chair. "Can't you see that in this relationship, all that you are ever going to do is give? What will you ever get back? Love is a two-way affair. If all you wanted was a piece of ass, you can get that anywhere." He was becoming desperate, and maybe angry, although I wasn't sure.

"You don't understand, Dad. She has never been loved, not really loved. She has so much potential as a person, but she has been consumed her entire life by loathing and self-doubt. She never knew the kind of love that you guys gave us."

"So what you want to do is parent her?"

"Dad, once she realizes what it means to be loved, and once she feels loved, all her insecurities will disappear and she will shine."

"I still don't get it. You are marrying her out of pity? How long will it take until she gets it? What if it takes a lifetime?"

"I know that she loves me. She makes me feel like my love is worth something. The whole thing is very intense."

"You know, you are so much like your mother. You take in the weak of the world and end up getting screwed."

"Are you saying that Mom ended up getting screwed? She married you, didn't she?"

"You know what I mean. Your mother can be irrational sometimes."

"Then why did you marry her?"

"I took time to get to know her and her family."

"Tell me, Dad, who is happier? You or Mom?"

"Mom and I are not the point. We don't even know Michelle's parents. . . ."

"That is something that I can take care of," I said, grateful to end the discussion.

I called Michelle and told her that we had to set up a meeting between our parents. They were so different. The religion of fish on Fridays was about to meet the religion of haute cuisine and vintage wine.

I set the meeting up for a Saturday afternoon, when Michelle's mother was not teaching class and my father would have wound down from the week's work. Her father uncharacteristically wore a tie and my father characteristically did as well. Their greetings were respectful but awkward. We left my house, to allow the future in-laws to get to know one another, and went back to hers. When we got to the house we wondered what they were saying. We role-played each other's parents, accentuating their idiosyncrasies, laughing nervously all the while. Her parents were there for hours before they eventually returned.

"We were honest and they were cordial. You have nice parents."

I was relieved, but they wouldn't say more. I didn't believe that my father had not put up a fight.

When I got home my father was sitting in his armchair. He was tugging at his chin, staring into space the way he does when he has something important to think about. I knew that he had been waiting for me. He held his hands together as if in prayer.

"Anthony, I know that your mind is made up. I want you just to spend some time thinking about how mentally ill she is. She tried to commit suicide. She is impulsive and unpredictable. And more than that, they are a family without God. She is going to need a lifetime of treatment. You are not going to marry a life partner but somebody who is going to need your care for the rest of her life. If you still decide that you are going to marry her, I will not stand in your way. But I strongly disapprove. Please think about it. Your mother and I truly love you."

I kissed him and hugged him. "Thanks, Dad."

"Okay," he said, resigned. "We'll get through it somehow."

I felt relieved, intensely relieved. I wanted to put his feelings out of my mind. I phoned Michelle. "Hey, Squirrel, let's celebrate." I had started calling her Squirrel for the way that she tucked herself into bed at night. She took the duvet and wrapped it around her body, then covered her head so that only her face and hands, holding the duvet, were visible, like a squirrel peering out of a hole in a tree. "Squirrels need a lot of love and a lot of warmth," she had instructed me. "I am going to be your squirrel."

We decided to make an unofficial and surprise announcement of our engagement to our close friends at a favorite restaurant. After the first round of drinks were served, I stood up and said, "Michelle and I have decided to get married. If you will raise your glass to Michelle." All of her friends erupted into laughter and joy, congratulating her heartily. My friends congratulated me as well, but not with the usual happiness associated with such an occasion. After a few more drinks, my friends warmed up to the idea more, but the drink also loosened their inhibitions. Gary was the most critical.

I had known Gary since the day we met at registration on the first day of medical school. Now, after graduation, we were able to reflect on the entire course of our journey, from pre-meds to qualified doctors. We had done so much together between studying, partying, playing bridge, and traveling to foreign lands during vacations. One time we decided to run the London Marathon together. Anybody who ran it in under four-and-a-half hours would get a medal and, even more important, would qualify for the infamous fifty-eight-mile Comrades Marathon in South Africa. After I had finished the race, I went back to look for Gary, who was still on the course. I looked at the race clock and it showed four hours and nineteen minutes. I ran out of the stadium and found him a mile from the finish line, not wanting to go on.

"Come on, Gary. Eleven minutes. You can do it!"

"I'm done. My legs are cramping, I'm hungry, and I had to stop to take a dump a mile back. There is no way. Now I just want to finish."

I knew that this was not true. He had been so set on finishing in under the required time that he had taken bets at school.

"Gary, you are going to run if I have to boot you across the

49

finish line." He laughed and started to trot. "Come on. A little faster; you're nearly there." We were nearing the stadium. "Gary, you have wanted this so badly, you will be so upset with yourself if you don't do it. You have been suffering for nearly four-and-a-half hours. Five minutes more won't kill you now." We entered the stadium. "A quarter mile, Gary. You have two-and-a-half minutes." The race marshal told me to get off the course, as I had already finished. Gary was on willpower alone. He collapsed across the finish line. His time was four hours, twenty-nine minutes, and fifty-six seconds. He had made it; the officials gave him his medal as the medics helped him to the recovery tent.

Gary and I had been together during our entire medical training. We understood the things that mattered to each other. At the restaurant that evening, he pulled me aside. "We are happy for you, if you are, but I know you. You never wanted this. Your dream will end. Remember that book you gave me? *Illusions* by Richard Bach? She isn't your soul mate. Yes, she is gorgeous, but her head is screwed up."

"Gary, I invited you here not to fight. I want you to be happy for me and for us. Her head is something that I understand. She is more alive than anyone that I have ever known."

"Just how alive is she? She nearly killed herself."

"Gary, get serious. We'll all die someday, but I'm telling you life with her is living."

"I am serious, my friend, but this is something that I see you are going to have to work out on your own." He ordered another drink. Eventually somebody drove him home. The dissent had ended.

The next morning Michelle woke up earlier than usual.

"There is just one last thing left to do before our formal party. I want a ring," she said. "A ring will make it official. I want to show it off."

"And you will have one. Let's go look today."

We cruised the jewelry stores in Bal Harbour, looking at the diamonds in their display cabinets. "God, can you ever imagine wearing one of those tiny pieces of shit," she said derisively of a smaller stone.

It bothered me that the size of the diamond meant so much to her. She knew that my father disapproved of the wedding and that he would not help me in this endeavor. I would pay for the ring myself. In my pre-internship year I had been paid a "travel stipend" of a hundred dollars a month—hardly enough to cover the cost of a large diamond.

As if she had read my mind, she said, "Baby, I know what you are giving up to do this for me, but I want you to know that I will always be able to look at it when you are not with me and know just how much you care, just how much you sacrificed. The ring will be a way of keeping you in my mind."

Later that day her mother told me that they had a relative in the jewelry business who would get me something at cost.

Michelle got her ring.

twelve

I enjoy being in situations that make me laugh so hard and long that my stomach hurts and I seriously worry about bladder control. I have always found humor to be a great reliever of stress. Other than studying, the two things that got me through six years of medical school were friendships and laughter.

We had a very serious colleague in our second-year class. She had recently moved to the United States from France. She told us that she was serious only because she had to concentrate on the lectures, as she had a difficult time understanding English. During human dissection, a course that lasted a year and involved four medical students dissecting in its entirety a donated human cadaver, she would complain bitterly when the body she was examining varied in the slightest from the pictures in the anatomy book we were using. One evening, on the day before we were to begin the examination of the intestines, we snuck into the dissection hall, removed a small section of bowel from our cadaver, and stitched it onto the bowel of her cadaver. The next day all hell erupted from the neighboring table as she ran around shouting that her book had nothing about extra bits of bowel attached to the gut. The senior anatomist teaching the course quickly discovered the prank and gave a stern lecture on the need to respect these human remains. Later our French colleague was able to laugh at the incident, and she stopped taking herself so seriously.

I had chosen a six-year M.D./Ph.D. program. The third year was the last purely academic year. At the end of that year we learned how to suture up a wound. We practiced this skill on oranges, which have a "give" similar to human skin. After we were done with our exams, Gary decided that the time had come for me to learn to surf.

"This beach will be good because the waves are not so big. A lot of beginners start here," he assured me. We paddled out to the waves. "If you want to get beyond the waves, you have to push the nose of the board under the break," he continued.

While he was showing me the technique of ducking under a breaking wave, one of the other beginners accidentally rammed the point of his surfboard into Gary's protruding rear-end. He screamed in pain and turned white. The surfer and I held on to Gary's board and paddled him to shore. Fortunately, we were able to get him seen at a beachfront clinic.

"So you guys are med students?" asked the attending doctor. We confirmed that we had just finished third year, so he offered me the needle and thread. "Why don't you suture up your friend?"

"What do you think, Gary?" I asked him.

"*C'est la vie*," he replied in his usual relaxed way. Gary lay on his stomach as I cleaned the wound and prepared the needle.

"Okay, here goes," I warned him, inexpertly inserting the needle into the edge of the cut.

"Youch!" he shouted, nearly jumping off the table. "What the hell was that?" The attending doctor came into the room.

"What happened?" Then he noticed the unopened vial of

anesthetic lying in the suture tray. "Don't you think that he'll need some of this?" he laughed. This being my first experience on a living human subject, I hadn't thought of it. The orange and the cadaver had never complained. After that incident, my friendship with Gary was sealed, and we would spend many poststudy hours playing bridge and drinking our favorite Napa Cabernet Sauvignon.

Aside from Gary and my bridge-playing, wine-drinking friends, Aaron was my closest confidante. I trusted him, literally, with my life. Together we had signed up for, and completed, a parachute jump. He was a restless adventurer, never content with a predictable daily schedule. We had started at medical school together, but halfway through he quit to go and hike in Nepal. For him it was always about the experience.

Aaron was an excellent athlete, and we had spent many an hour running through the streets of the Gables and on the beach, chatting about girlfriends, baseball, movies, black holes, and the solutions to life's problems. After months of training with him, he proposed running the Western States 100-miler. In June of my fourth year we ran the race together. I finished the monster course, climbing and descending over rough, barely broken trails from Squaw Valley and Placer High in just over twenty-three hours, and lived to tell the tale.

Although Aaron had an opinion on many things, he was always nonjudgmental about my personal choices, unlike Gary, who told me exactly what he thought of everything I did. Perhaps I should have asked Aaron early on what he thought about my relationship with Michelle, but because I didn't expect an opinion, I didn't ask him. I had left one of my closest confidantes without a voice.

Dating was a frivolous affair for many of us during medical school. There did not seem to be enough time or energy to commit to serious relationships. The nursing students and the medical students played the same game with one another, and usually after a few movies and a brief romance, each moved on. It was more difficult to date during the surgery rotations because of the long hours in the operating room and the frequency of the calls, so we all looked forward to the easier rotations like dermatology and ophthalmology.

It was the mix of study, friendship, and laughter that made it possible to get sanely through medical school, and even though I knew that the craziness and long hours would come to an end, I still looked forward to maintaining this balance long after school had ended.

thirteen

EARLY JUNE

After I had completed my final examinations at medical school, Michelle and I spent nearly all our time together. There were two nights when she told me that she couldn't make it to one of the many graduation parties, so I met up with friends instead. On both of those occasions she showed up at the party some time later, to my great delight.

"How did you know where we were?" I'd ask her.

"You weren't thinking that you could get away from me that easily, were you?" she'd laugh.

"As if I'd ever want to," I'd laugh with her. "Besides, I'm glad you came. I want everyone to know why I am so happy."

As graduation was over, we turned our attention to the engagement party. Michelle's mother had set the menu, so we were instructed to order the chairs, tables, stemware, and flatware. The running around and preparing for the party felt in some ways like running away for me. I was distracted from thinking about what I was doing, and from my father's antipathy. I knew he felt that I hadn't given his earlier warning much thought. In the mornings I stayed in bed until after he had left for work so that I wouldn't have to face him over the breakfast table and deal with his objections. In the evenings I left before he returned home, and I left my bedroom window open so that I could get in at night. I knew how much he was opposed to what I was about to do, and I also knew that there was no convincing him of the fact that I had made a decision that I was prepared to live by. He was the immovable object, and Michelle the irresistible force. I could not tolerate the tension between, on the one hand, his total rejection of her and what he felt she represented, and on the other, her need to not have me fail and abandon her. I could not stand just how judgmental and preachy he was. I knew that he didn't approve, but he had made my relationship with him unbearable by his contempt. I had made my choice, and she was my future. I felt that in time he would understand.

During the day I would be with Michelle at her house. We helped her mother with the garden, with polishing the silver, and with ensuring that the crystal wine glasses were free of blemish. There was not a spot in the house that did not receive attention. "Great food demands a great presentation," her mother insisted.

Soon the day was upon us.

The party began in the late afternoon of a warm summer's day. The sky was an immaculate blue—even that detail seemed to have been taken care of. The lawn was manicured, without so much as a single dandelion to spoil it. The garden bloomed with white dendrobium, deep pink peonies, and petunias. The pool obediently mirrored the blue of the sky. At the door the guests were greeted with Veuve-Clicquot champagne in Baccarat flutes. Pockets of people began to form and dissolve as we moved from one "Congratulations!" to the next.

My parents had not yet arrived, so I numbed my anxiety

with Chardonnay. When this did not help, I took an offered cigarette with no remorse. When still they had not arrived, anxiety became anger at their rudeness, but even that passed, and by the time they showed up, the party had swung into full disinhibition. The fading rays of the late-afternoon sun invited all for a last look at the garden.

My father wore a solemn suit to this solemn occasion. He sought out a glass of wine to numb his pain, and then sought out Gary to commiserate with; but other than this pessimistic couple, all the other guests seemed to be enjoying themselves. Michelle's therapist had been invited, and upon arrival the therapist cornered me and commended me on how well Michelle was doing. "You're all she talks about in therapy. You have surprised all of us with your tenacity. You'll need it. Michelle is one tough girl." I wondered if she was warning me but could see no hint of this in her face.

The loud drone of relaxed chatter filled the evening. Laughter and merriment drowned out any lingering feelings of doubt. An occasional knife clinked on the side of an empty wineglass to propose a toast, and we cheered and laughed. Her father spoke of how much they had come to love me and how happy Michelle seemed to be. "I don't recall her ever having been so content with life and with herself." My father, uncharacteristically but not unexpectedly, made no speech. I filled the silence.

"When two people meet and have feelings for each other, it is usual that each shows the other all the niceness about themselves. Seldom do we bare our weaknesses in the initial encounters, for fear of driving the other away. It is later that these flaws are revealed and the core of the relationship is truly tested.

When I met Michelle, as all of you know, she was in the hospital, hopeless and in pain. It is easy to love someone who is perfect, but Michelle allowed me to share in her weakest moment, and Squirrel, I love you for that, and nothing will ever break that love apart."

Hooting and whistling accompanied Michelle's passionate kiss.

"Everything is going to be just perfect, I promise you," she whispered.

fourteen

My internship would begin next month, in July, and Michelle was coming with me. I had been matched with my first choice, Taos Medical Center, located in that northern New Mexico town. Taos is situated more than two thousand miles from Miami on a high-desert mesa at the foot of the spectacular Sangre de Cristo Mountains. It was two thousand miles away from my parents and Michelle's, two thousand miles away from managed care and crowded emergency rooms, two thousand miles away from big-city violence and full parking lots.

My car was an old red Ford Mustang, and getting it ready for the trip was as much an act of mercy as it was a necessity. Among other, more pressing problems, the muffler didn't quite muffle, but my medical school loans were mounting, so I decided to wait for my first paycheck before getting a new one.

Two weeks before we were to leave, I received a call from the director of housing at the medical center, informing me that she had arranged a studio apartment for me in their doctors' apartment block and that the caretaker would have a key. I told her that I would need a larger apartment as I was just engaged and that my fiancée would be staying with me. "But you did not indicate that on your application form," she said.

"Well, it was all rather sudden," I explained.

"We reserve all the bigger apartments for the married couples and those with kids. I am sorry, but housing is tight for the doctors. Also, the couples with kids complain that the single docs have too many parties. If you would like, we could look for something in town. We can't guarantee anything, though."

The original housing offer had sounded ideal, as it offered all the amenities that a sleep-, exercise-, and food-deprived intern could ask for. Moreover, it was on the hospital grounds and would be far less expensive than a private rental, so a move into town was not appealing.

"What assholes," said Michelle. Her mind worked quickly. We had previously agreed to have a traditional wedding after my internship was over. "Let's just tell them that we're married."

"I told her that we are engaged, and that we were getting married next year. She said that there was no way that they could provide a bigger apartment unless we are married or have kids."

"They want us to be married? Let's just go down to the courthouse and get married. We won't tell anybody, so next year we'll still get our wedding and for now we will have a bigger apartment."

Our relationship had reached a sudden, unexpected, and critical juncture. I had felt that the decision to wait a year before we got married made sense so that we could see what living together would bring, especially during a year of internship with multiple demands on my time. Also, I wanted to show my father that I had spent time thinking about what I was doing, to show him that Michelle and I could be a couple and ultimately get his blessing. But if we did not go through with Michelle's plan, she would not be able to live with me in Taos, and there was no way our relationship would last. I knew that my father would never help us with the rent for a private apartment, and her parents had already agreed to help us furnish whatever place we got.

"I don't want to ask them for more," said Michelle decisively. "But you know what? I need to be with you. I can't stay here in Miami and you there. If you abandon me, I'll just have to look for somebody else. I can't be alone. You know that."

I had made a commitment to her. I was terrified by the thought that she would leave me for somebody else. I had no choice. I would not abandon her. I telephoned the local justices-of-the-peace, but due to the short notice, nobody in our town could marry us. Michelle then called and found a minister in the next town who told us that their civil court performed weddings on Wednesdays and that he had just had a cancellation. He would be glad to submit our names instead. We immediately took the offer. All we needed was two witnesses and twenty-five dollars. I imagined what my father would say: "A marriage without God is not a marriage."

Because Aaron knew me as well as he did, I finally asked him what he thought of my relationship with Michelle. He told me that he felt that my romance was just another adventure. "You live the thrill of risk and the challenge of things that most people would never undertake. Just like jumping out of an airplane or running the Western States 100-miler, the experience will change your life no matter what the outcome," he assured me.

"Okay, my friend, I want you to be part of this experience, just like all the other crazy moments we have shared. Michelle and I were going to wait a year to get married, but we have to do it immediately in order to get housing in Taos," I told him.

62

"I want you to be my witness and best man. I'm getting married at the courthouse. You have to be there by eleven on Wednesday, and please Aaron, don't tell anybody. If my father ever finds out, it will kill him."

"I have a meeting that ends at ten-thirty. I'll be there on time, and don't worry, no one will know, at least not from me."

I had many doubts over the next few days. Sometimes the doubts were the realization that I didn't really know her, sometimes a sense of having failed my family, but mostly a growing feeling that I was losing my sense of judgment. Worse was that the only people I wanted to hear from were those who would validate my decision; any other choice would be showing Michelle that I wasn't able to make this final and all-encompassing act of love. Surely this would prove to her my level of commitment for eternity.

The reality of what I was about to do made me reflect on the events of the past few months. Michelle and I had known each other for four months. We had been engaged for two weeks and were to be married in a few days. I didn't believe I could put the wedding on hold. It would have shattered Michelle's fragile but growing sense of hope and trust in me. But I dreaded going through with the wedding a year before I had intended, and just for the sake of getting a larger apartment. Our relationship had not yet been put to any significant test. Finally I decided that there was no choice for me but to stand by my conviction that flooding her with love would be the force that would eventually drown out any doubt she could possibly have.

Wednesday morning arrived, and we got to court shortly before the eleventh hour. A receptionist showed us to a small, sparsely decorated, windowless room that had a large, formal-looking chair and solid wood table at one end and four folding chairs leaning against the wall at the other. Florida's state flag hung proudly alongside the Stars and Stripes behind the table.

"Just take the two middle chairs, and when your witnesses arrive, tell them to take the other two chairs," said the receptionist.

Michelle's friend Kathy arrived, but shortly after eleven there was still no sign of Aaron. An elderly woman peered around the door. "Sorry dears, we are going to have to start. The next couple is waiting." I asked her to wait for another minute but Aaron did not show. Instead the judge walked in with jeans showing under an ill-fitting gown, carrying a large, red-leather-bound book.

"We are going to have to start. Is your witness here?" Aaron had still not arrived.

"You will need a witness. There is a secretary pool down the hall. Ask one of them to stand in for your friend." A kind-looking, somewhat bemused woman in her mid-thirties offered to be witness. "It's the first time that I have ever been a best man," she laughed, and then the ceremony was conducted.

By the power invested in the judge, we were pronounced husband and wife. "Please sign here," he said, opening up the red book, "and pay the cashier on the way out." And then he was gone. In the waiting room sat a young couple, hands and eyes interlocked, waiting for their ten minutes in court. We paid the cashier and I looked at my watch: 11:08. There was still no sign of Aaron, so after a few more minutes we left.

Kathy had a cold bottle of Moet waiting for us in her Volkswagen Beetle, and she offered to be our chauffeur for the day. She drove us to a trendy French restaurant while we polished off the champagne in the back the car.

At lunch we sat in a secluded booth and ordered Chardonnay by the bottle, which we accompanied with oysters by the plateful. Then, hardly needing a main course, we ordered that too. Michelle placed an oyster in her mouth and then took my hand, sucking on my fingers with the oyster, still smooth, in her mouth. She then took my hand and placed it gently between her thighs and slowly rubbed herself on it. She reached orgasm just as the waiter brought our dessert, a slice of Black Forest cake.

"Another plate of oysters," said Michelle.

"After the chocolate, madam?" queried the waiter.

"Yes," Michelle laughed. "But then wait twenty minutes before bringing the coffee."

fifteen

The next morning I awoke severely hungover. "I'm married," I said to myself, as if this were a sudden revelation. I decided to go for a jog. Jogging had been my mainstay exercise, and I had managed to maintain my weight at around 170 pounds for the past few years. But with the excitement of a new romance, the restaurants, the year-end parties, and Michelle's mother's cooking, jogging had slipped down on my priority list. That morning I stood on the scale, and 180 pounds stared me straight in the eye. I moved the scale around to make sure there was not an error, but the weight did not change. My new, food-rich lifestyle had taken its toll. I had to put a quick stop to this.

"I am off, darling," I told Michelle, who lay burrowed in her duvet.

"Where to?" she asked.

"For a run. Look at this: I am getting fat." I wobbled my gut in front of her, laughing.

"So what?"

"What do you mean?"

"So what if you're getting fat?"

"I need to lose some weight."

"Who are you trying to impress?"

"Nobody; it's just a healthy thing to do. Anyway, my pants are getting tight."

"What's wrong with all you men? You think that you have to have rock hard bodies to get the chicks. That's not what women want. That's not what I want. Anyway, there is no one to impress now that you have me. I want you to take care of me. I want you to make so much money that I never have to work and we can go to restaurants whenever we want. I don't want some pansy prancing around in his tights."

"What's gotten into you? This isn't some vanity trip. I'm just going for a run."

"So it is more important to you to go for a run than to be with me?"

"What are you talking about? I am with you. I'll be back in half an hour."

Michelle took a half-empty wineglass from the nightstand and smashed it to the ground. "What the hell are you doing to me? You promised me that you would never leave." I shuddered and stepped back from her. She started to cry. "You are doing that now. You promised that you would never leave me."

I went to hold her.

"I promise you, baby, that I will never leave you. If it means so much to you, I won't go for the run today. It's no big deal, but I do have to start getting some exercise."

"Just promise me that you will never leave me."

"I promise," I said sincerely.

"Let's go lie by the pool. I want to bring you something."
She disappeared, and then returned sometime later carrying two

large bowls of ice cream that she had decorated with cherries and a banana to make a smiling face.

"I love you. I promise, when we get to Taos we'll start going for walks together."

"I love you too, and that's a great idea!" I reassured her.

sixteen

MID-JUNE

"I have something for you," Michelle proclaimed triumphantly one morning.

"What is it?" I wondered.

"Close your eyes," she said playfully, then covered my eyes with her hand to be sure that I didn't peek. She led me into the hallway and faced me toward the far end of the hall. "Keep them closed," she ordered, and then removed her hand from my face. I heard her walk away. "Okay, now open them." On the far wall a sheet covered the clear outline of a large frame. She pulled the sheet off the painting.

From behind the sheet appeared an oil painting on canvas. She had had it framed in an intricate solid-wood frame. I stared at the painting for a long time, to take it all in. Michelle had created a Chagall-like flower arrangement that overflowed with yellow lilies, white chrysanthemums, blue irises, yellow-and-white alstroemeria, and baby's breath flowing from a rustic clay pot. The background was a fiery sunset red that made the piece look larger than it was.

"That could hang in any gallery anywhere in the world. It is magnificent," I said, finally. "When did you have time to do it?"

"I started on it soon after we met. I had a lot of time to work on it during your exams. I wanted to show you that I had been thinking of you all this time. Also, I'm sorry about the other day."

I was sure that the mind that had created such art was close to genius. Van Gogh and Michelangelo had been excused for their madness. I was not in their presence, but Michelle was as close as I would get to artistic greatness. Perhaps she needed her rage to create. It was a small price to pay for such beauty, I thought at the time.

seventeen

The next few days were spent preparing the last details of the trip. The tension at my parents' home was intolerable. My father hoped that I would change my decision. He asked my friends to speak to me, but my mind was made up. He did not know it, but Michelle and I were now legally married. I could not wait to leave.

Soon the day arrived, and with the car packed we said our good-byes to her parents and drove to see my parents. After she had wished Michelle luck, my mother hugged her and cried. My father hugged me and said softly, "Just remember that no matter what happens, we will always be there for you." We got in the car and Michelle turned on the radio. Meat Loaf was singing "Bat Out of Hell."

We had planned to do the trip in three days and drove up I-95 to I-10 West, spending an uneventful and thoroughly exhaustion-relieving night in Tallahassee. The next morning, up early, we continued through to Mobile, Alabama, where we stopped for lunch at Butch Cassidy's and completely stuffed ourselves with burgers. This, together with a couple of beers, made a local motel our next stop.

"I need a room for me and my wife for the night."

Michelle pinched me and giggled. "That's the first stranger

you've ever introduced me to as your wife," she whispered seductively in my ear. The ponytailed desk attendant looked at Michelle and then at me and winked. "Here's a special room for you two." As Michelle turned her back, he winked again. "Enjoy."

The room was their equivalent of the bridal suite, with mirrored walls, a red-flannel-covered bed with the potential to vibrate, for additional cost, and a hot tub. After turning on the hot tub, we made love under a lukewarm shower, lay in the tub for half an hour, then fell asleep without activating the vibration option. After a three-hour nap, I paid the bill and received a predictable wink. We set off again, behind schedule.

We arrived in Shreveport, Louisiana, a little after midnight and found another welcoming motel, with a pipe-smoking, white-haired, older man attendant and a reasonably comfortable queen-sized bed. The next morning we rose fairly early, thanks to the unbearable whining of a family of hungry mosquitoes. We continued on I-20 to Dallas, then north toward Oklahoma City. There we headed west on I-40 and stopped for the night in Amarillo. The next morning, we awoke for our final stretch. We toured around the treasure that is Amarillo and left the city late, then drove through the suburbs and on to the stretches of open road between the towns, and then into the desert. The greens of watered lawns faded into dry summer browns as we entered arid New Mexico.

The long trip was passed with long naps, painless chatter, and talk of our life together over the next few years as well as in the more immediate future. But there were also moments when Michelle was clearly thinking about her struggle. After a half-hour stretch of quiet, with only a contemporary-rock station to fill the silence, Michelle held my hand and said, "Do you know how difficult it is for me to change? But you know what? How easy is it for you to change? Do you really think that we have the freedom of choice that your father so easily preaches? Do you think that I choose my fear that you will abandon me, that I choose my depression? I can't stand it. If I had a knife, I would cut it out. But you can't change either. Think about it. Try to choose to act differently. You are so predictable. That's not bad, we all are, but let's not fucking fool ourselves that we have the freedom of choice. Change is extremely hard if not impossible."

I loved these refreshing moments of insight. I knew few people who so deeply looked into themselves, and yet sadly this knowledge and these insights didn't seem to help her, other than in knowing that maybe she needed therapy, or at least she needed me for now. I realized that I was mistaking her unpredictable behavior for apparent freedom of choice. This made her appear deliciously freer and sexier that anyone I had ever known. Ultimately there was no such freedom. Her emotional intensity was the uncontrollable manifestation of her occasionally chaotic mind.

The alien rock formations, gifts of the desert, broke the monotony of the straight shimmering blacktop. The car had no air-conditioning, and the fan blew hot engine air back into the car. After we had reached no particular place, we stopped, stripped down to our shorts, and walked out onto the desert sands. Our bodies glistened with the moisture of sweat. We danced deliriously in the sun to the sound of the distant car radio. A lizard appeared, then quickly darted back into the shade of a small rock. We headed back to the car. The ice that had kept the Coke cold was now tepid water at the bottom of the ice chest, but even that brought some relief as we poured the water over ourselves.

We continued the drive through the late afternoon and watched as the sun finally set behind a large mesa. Mercifully, the night came quickly and took the heat away, even bringing with it an occasional breeze. Suddenly over a rise, the lights of Santa Fe appeared. The familiar sign of a Holiday Inn promised air-conditioned rooms and ice-cold beer. We settled for both.

The next morning we continued west and reached a gravel road with a sign that promised to take a hundred miles off the trip. The surface looked to be in good condition, so we left the paved national road and headed into the brush. Twenty miles into the desert we realized how absolutely alone we were. The only sign of civilization was the ever-deteriorating road we were driving on. After a long silence, Michelle said suddenly, "This is what it is like sometimes. I am alone in an empty world that I can't even recognize. It's better to be dead." The times that she was able to reflect on her life were rare. Usually, after she had had an outburst, she would yell and shout about how miserable her life was, and how she would rather be dead. This moment was different. Unprovoked and reflective, she told it the way that it was for her. I put my hand on her bare knee and gave her a reassuring squeeze.

After a while the road rejoined the interstate. The gravel road had been in such poor condition that we had added another two hours to the trip, but eventually, after another hundred miles, we reached the outer limits of Taos. A gas station attendant directed us to the other end of the town where the medical center was. "Twenty thousand people live in the area," he said, almost proudly. We continued on to the hospital and found the doctors' living quarters well sign-posted. An older, heavyset, slow-moving Latino woman answered my knock on the caretaker's door.

"Apartment 2B?" I asked.

She pointed us to some stairs. "My name is Dulcia Morales. You go up that way and I'll take the elevator. It's my knee." She met us at the top of the stairs and led us to our new home. The apartment had two bedrooms, a living room, a kitchen, and a bathroom. The place was empty except for two single beds separated by a small bookstand and a refrigerator in the kitchen.

"Where's the air conditioner? Where's the double bed?" asked Michelle.

"None of the apartments are air-conditioned," said the caretaker.

"How do people take the heat?" I persisted, perspiring.

"This is the desert. We have always lived with the heat. If you want an air conditioner, you can go into town and buy one. And you can get a double bed there too, if you want one. Listen, you have to turn on the refrigerator. It's been off for a couple of days since the last doctor left, but don't worry, I cleaned it myself."

We moved the bookstand and pushed the beds together, then left for town to buy bedding for two singles and food to stock the refrigerator, and to look for an air conditioner.

The first two tasks were a success. The last proved impossible, as the summer's early heat had ensured a complete depletion of any stock. An order would take a couple of weeks.

Instead we bought a large water-cooled fan. That first night I dreamt that I had built a sauna in the middle of the desert and had sat in it fully clothed, unable to get out.

The next day was the last free day before my internship began. We woke early. Michelle filled the ice trays with water and placed them in the freezer. "I'll show you why later," she said suggestively. We then drove into town to get our bearings. We stopped at the bank to open an account and get a loan in order to buy furniture for the apartment. Michelle found a classic dining room table with four chairs in unfinished oak, so we put our loan to immediate use.

Happy with our purchase, we next found the only European-style restaurant in town. It offered fresh oysters, and we sat down to a plateful, accompanied by a chilled Zinfandel. Both had their desired effect, and we rushed back in the midday heat to an ice-cold bath, using the ice from the freezer. Michelle turned on the radio. Sinatra was singing "For Once in My Life." She sang along, "I've got someone who needs me . . ."

Finally, frozen and lightheaded, we warmed our bodies in love and whispered to each other that we would overcome all obstacles and be together forever.

eighteen

MONDAY, JULY 1
TAOS, NEW MEXICO

I arrived early at the hospital to meet my colleagues. All but one of the new interns had graduated from American medical schools. One woman had studied in Russia and barely spoke English, but she appeared just as excited and nervous as the rest of us. "I just passed the ECFMGs"—the foreign-graduate medical examinations—"and my English test," she reassured me. The attending staff divided us into groups of two and handed us a schedule for the rest of the year. I also received a pager and, oddly, it was only after attaching it to my belt that I felt fully confident that I was an official doctor.

The paging system that the hospital used was a voice-activated system with a ten-mile radius. It immediately announced the caller's message. The hospital operator would preface the message with "Doctor," and all nearby could hear. "Doctor, you are needed in Ward Three-B to replace a leaking catheter." The first few times I looked around to see whether people had noticed, but after a few days the pager became more of a nuisance than a status symbol. In truth, though, I was terrified of the new responsibility, unsure of whether anything that I had learned in medical school would be of practical use.

My first assignment was a two-month stint in a surgery rotation. This required my being at the hospital by six in the morning and getting home by six at night. I spent the day in the operating room with one of the senior fellows or staff surgeons. Every third night I was on call for the surgery service, and I slept, though barely so, in the doctor's quarters at the hospital.

Michelle soon began to hate life in Taos. She was unable to escape from her own insecurities through the activity that had filled her life in Miami. She could no longer spend time cruising the malls, having coffees in quaint coffee shops, and talking to friends over lunch, for there were no malls or coffee shops or friends. With these gone, she had little to do but think about her life. The solitude forced her to face the fears that haunted her most: her fear of abandonment and her fear of being alone. The loneliness magnified her feeling of emptiness. She knew that this lifestyle would eventually make her snap. She would lose control and lash out, then feel embarrassed for having done so. She always hated herself after losing control. She so hated that part of her psyche that could not control the anger that the thought of dying during those moments was, for her, relieving. "If I killed myself I wouldn't have to live with myself, and I wouldn't end up hurting so many people."

"I know that you hate being here, but you aren't threatened here," I reassured her. "I have no family and friends to take me away from you. You have me all to herself."

"Yes, but your job takes you away from me for twelve hours a day, sometimes more. And you aren't the only one without friends. Imagine what it is like for me just having to sit here and wait." She had lost her motivation to paint, but one

Saturday afternoon we found a private pottery class. She dropped out after one lesson. "You just want me to do pottery lessons so that you can spend some time away from me. It's your way of driving me away," she told me one day. "In any case, I really hate it here. There is nothing to do. I can't even get a job." She was right about that because for many of the service jobs a proficiency in Spanish was necessary for employment in a state that still proudly displayed its historic connection with colonial Spain.

"You knew that when we moved here, yet you decided to make the move in any case, to be here with me. I wish you had learned Spanish in school back home," I chided her. The reality of the dreary day-to-day life in the desert had killed the motivation that she had shown before the trip. She spent her time in the apartment reading and waiting for me to come home. In the evenings we ate out, feasting on the new experience of Southwestern cuisine. One night we found an eccentric restaurant run by a large German man and his tiny wife. Both shared a booming laugh and readily accepted an invitation to share a beer, so they invited us for dinner again, but the novelty of eating there soon wore off. The only cinema in town changed their feature every three weeks, but fortunately there was a good video-rental store a few blocks from the apartment.

On the weekends that I was not on call we would go exploring the desert or Taos Mountain. "There is something about Taos, which we tell to all the new people," warned Dulcia after we had recounted one of our trips. "If Taos Mountain likes you, times will be good and that which you seek will be found here. If it doesn't, you'll be spit out like the used shell of a piñon nut. The relationship with Taos is two-way." Dulcia's style was generally straightforward and welcoming, but her warning made me shudder. In any case, she was a walking travel guide to the area.

The day trips cheered Michelle up a lot. She would prepare a picnic basket full of cheese, cold cuts, bread, and wine, and we would set off to discover a new aspect of the desert. One afternoon we unexpectedly found a small lake, a feature that did not appear on our map. It was more of a pond, though a hand-painted sign humorously identified it as the LARGEST BODY OF WATER IN THE TAOS AREA. A big rock at its edge made it an ideal place to hide from the heat and enjoy a picnic. It was under that rock that we got down to the work of really knowing each other. We would talk and fight for hours about our dreams and ourselves. This was the process that I had expected to complete during our year of living together, before our sudden marriage.

There were two fundamental areas where we disagreed. The first was that I wanted children and she did not.

"I am sick. I can't even take care of myself. How do you expect me to take care of a child? I want to be your baby. I want you to take care of me like I was your child. Unconditional love is what I need. I love you so much that I just can't stand the idea of sharing your love with anybody else. I want it all to myself. I would go crazy. Maybe I'd even hurt the baby. I know how I get. Why should a baby suffer because of how I am?" she argued.

"When you finally begin to truly believe just how much I love you, then maybe we can think about it again. It doesn't have to be now."

"I don't know why people want children. There are already so many in the world and all they do is cry and wet and you can't enjoy yourself. We haven't even started to enjoy our life together and already you are talking about having children and throwing it all away. I want my life to be mine for a while. I have never had that except for now and I want that feeling for a long time."

The second thing that we disagreed on was the importance of family, at least my family. For Michelle it was intolerable that I could love anybody but her. She saw them as a threat to my feelings for her. I could love her and only her. The more I loved my family, the more she hated them.

"It is a different kind of love, built over years of being a family. I love you as my wife and my companion and nothing will break that."

"Your family is your past. I am your present and your future. I don't want to hear about your past and your family," she screamed one morning under the rock by the lake.

I could understand why she did not want to have children, but her hatred of my family was intolerable. She attacked them because she knew that she could get me to respond when no other of her provocations would. They were my vulnerability. It became a cycle, her venom toward them and my defending them, which in turn enraged her all the more. She could not tolerate the possibility that I could have any happiness outside of being with her. In her eyes everything in my past was no longer part of me.

"I don't want to hear about your life before you met me. It doesn't exist. It is not a part of us. If you were so happy with your family," she would add in a sarcastic, goading tone, "then why are you with me?"

"I was happy then and I am happy now. This is a different stage in my life."

The more we didn't see or hear from my family, the more fearsome and loathsome they became in her mind. Her hatred of them was like a cancer that grew unabated. Without being with them she could not see them as good in any way. She saw them as trying to destroy us and destroy her at every turn. But then when my mother would call, speaking to her would ground Michelle. Michelle could feel my mother's compassion. "Maybe your mother is not so bad, but it's your father. What has he ever done for us?"

It was a lethal, double-edged blade. On the one hand she didn't want me to talk about my family and my past. She wanted me to have no identity outside of her. She feared that it would destroy us. "If you love them a little, you can't love me totally and completely, because some of your love is for them." On the other hand she could not tolerate the idea of me keeping any secrets from her. "How do you expect me never to talk to you about my family and my past but at the same time never to keep anything from you? How is that possible? I am who I am because of my past, my life experiences, everything. I love you because of my mother's love for me. I didn't grow up in a vacuum," I protested.

"That's your problem."

Once I received a letter from my brother, which I slipped into the pages of *The Hitchhiker's Guide to the Galaxy*. Michelle found it and tore the letter and the book to shreds.

"So how long have you been keeping this behind my back? I can't take your little secrets and your lies."

"You don't want to hear me tell you about them, and then when I don't you go crazy. What do you want me to do?"

I always had a terrible feeling at times like these. It was as if she had caught me with my hand in the cookie jar, after handing me the cookie jar. Her extreme insecurity and self-doubt were a malignancy that ate away at her sense of reason. She hated herself for her paranoia, yet she needed it. She believed that people eventually would always leave her. This fear tormented her constantly. She spent her days looking for hints to confirm this belief. Even the smallest disagreement turned into what she saw as the end of love.

"Everybody always leaves me in the end, don't you know that? I tell you all the time. You will too. How can anybody love me when I can't even love myself? I take the people that I love the most and I hurt them the most. I am so scared you will leave that I want to give you a reason to leave me. It is impossible to love me enough."

nineteen

Michelle's parents had been kind in giving us some money to make the transition to New Mexico easier. They called often to see how we were doing. Her mother always wanted to speak to me to see how Michelle was doing, and then she wanted to know if I was all right. It dawned on me that they sent money not just to make things easier for us, but easier for them. "Sure," her mother admitted. "It's a break for us too, not having her around. We can live a normal life, but she is still our daughter."

My parents, on the other hand, were not supportive. They still did not know that we were married. Michelle relished the idea that one day she would tell my father that his son had not only been deceitful, but that he had not been married in a church. My father did, however, make periodic phone calls and did so one morning about five weeks into the internship. Michelle answered the phone. I was in the bathroom shaving when I heard her say, "He doesn't want to talk to you." I suspected that it was my father and went into the bedroom to take the call.

"I don't give a shit what he is to you," Michelle continued. "He is my husband, you fucking asshole!"

"Dad?" I had grabbed the phone from her, but the line was

dead. I tried his home and work number, but he didn't answer at either place.

"He deserved it. He never liked me. What has he ever done for me to show me that he cares? What has he ever done for us? You are with me now. You have to give up your daddy. Don't fight it. He is a grown man. He can take it and so can you."

I felt the pain of his having found out that we were married. I was overwhelmed with sadness on my way to work and I cried, not with anger or frustration but with pity for myself and for being so stupid. I was certain that my father thought that he had lost me for good. I wanted to reach out and tell him that I would be okay and that I wouldn't allow this relationship to destroy me, or my love for him. I didn't know how to reach out.

I returned home that evening to find Michelle had prepared her favorite dinner, a pasta primavera with sautéed asparagus tips. The day had been particularly long in the operating room, as we had nearly lost a patient who ruptured his spleen in a car accident. I was in no mood to fight with Michelle, but she was conciliatory. She hugged me tightly. "I am sorry, baby. You know that I love you. I am sorry for the way that I am."

A week went by without anger. In order to make the apartment more attractive, we had decided to sponge paint the walls. This gave Michelle a creative task to do for us. She worked hard at it, and the tension that had grown between us after my father's phone call eased. Fights were inevitably followed by lovemaking. The passions were extreme. Anger turned to love so fully that it was difficult to imagine that there had ever been anger. For Michelle it was the only way to be sure that I really loved her. "I know that you love me because you still make love to me even after we have a fight." She was right. Her sorrow and embarrassment at her outbursts were real, and her attempts to control her anger so earnest that I knew she was trying for me, for herself, and for us. I had to remind myself that I had known that she was intense to the extreme in her experience of life, and that her struggle was my struggle. We would share anger, but we would also share love.

One morning, after a particularly hot night, the sticky air made us both irritable. Michelle was not happy, but I had to leave for work and had little time to listen and less to sympathize.

"Okay, I am off to rounds," I said indifferently.

"I just can't stand it here," she said.

"Look, this place is the way it is. It's not going to change. Why don't you see it for what it can offer you?" I headed for the door, picking up my lab coat on the way.

"What are you doing to me? Why are you leaving? I'm not doing well. Just stay a little while," she cried.

"We'll talk about it when I get back. I'm late."

"I swear, if you leave now I will kill myself." She sounded desperate.

"I am just going to do rounds. I'll be back in a couple of hours." I picked up my pager and left. As soon as I got into the car, my pager went off.

"Please come back." Her voice was altered electronically by the paging system and she sounded robot-like. I ignored her page and headed off to the hospital. "Please don't leave," she pleaded over the pager. She paged me three more times on my way in. Each time she was begging, imploring, beseeching that

I come back. I started rounds and my pager went off again. "Please call me." Her voice sounded thin yet chilling. She sounded desperate. I excused myself from rounds and called from the nursing station.

"What is it, babe, are you okay?"

"Please come home. I don't know what I've done. There is blood everywhere."

I excused myself from rounds and rushed home, then sprinted up the stairs to the apartment. The distinct smell of blood greeted me at the front door. I heard her crying, almost wailing, almost sobbing. She sounded profoundly alone. The crying was coming from the bathroom. The bathroom door was closed. I shuddered at the thought of what I would find. I pushed the door open and found her sitting in the bath. The walls and the floor were covered in blood. Her wrists were slit open and the blood flowed into the warm bath water. She was wearing a Mickey Mouse nightshirt, which was soaked with her blood and her tears. I was heartbroken to see her in so much misery. I realized then that I did not really understand her. The question I had asked myself those months earlier in Miami was still the question I was asking today. What was the pain she experienced that only death could alleviate? What caused such torment and such intolerable anguish? I had no answers. Instead, I held her close to me and cried with her. "I am so sorry, my baby. I'm so sorry."

I looked at her wrists. The cuts were mostly superficial, but numerous. I cleaned her arms and cuts with warm water, then bandaged her wrists with gauze. Finally, she spoke.

"Please promise me that you will never leave me," she begged.

87

"I promise that I will never leave you," I said, holding her tightly. I helped her back to the bedroom. She was pale and weakened by the loss of blood. Softly I whispered, "Baby, I need to go back to finish rounds. If you want you can come along. Maybe my job won't threaten you as much if you see what I do." She placed her head on my chest and nodded.

"What are you going to tell people when they see the bandages?" she asked.

"We'll tell them that you chafed them on the pottery wheel while you were molding clay."

Back at the hospital, she waited at the nursing station while I finished rounds. After that we went to the children's ward, where I was called in on a consult to monitor the progress of a four-year-old child who had been abandoned by his mother. He had been found close to death and taken to the hospital for treatment. He had developed a condition where his brain fluid could not easily flow through the brain, causing his head to swell to the size of a big pumpkin. His eyes bulged and he quickly tired when he tried to stand because of the weight of his head. The child, however, had a beaming smile that had endeared him to all the staff. He was waiting to be flown to St. Louis to have a procedure that would reduce the fluid build-up in his head. Michelle took immediate pity on the boy and gave him the box of M&M's that she had been eating.

As unpredictable as she was, Michelle always showed compassion to those whom she perceived to be less fortunate than she was. She never felt threatened by the sick or oppressed, and there were plenty of both in New Mexico. When she was with anyone more vulnerable than she herself was, a kind, puerile selflessness would show.

"You did great with that little kid. I can't believe that you don't want children," I said.

"He reminded me of me," she answered. "I wish that I could be cared for as much as he is. I *am* a baby. I *am* a child. Please don't forget that."

I felt exhausted that evening. I wondered what I was doing. I wondered what it was that I was trying to prove. I thought of all the choices that I made every day. Some of those choices, like smoking cigarettes and marijuana, not exercising, drinking too much, and eating too much fat, led me closer to death. Other choices, like choosing love and honesty over hate and mistrust, had set me free. I felt that I had a choice to make. I could choose to get out of the relationship at that point, but I convinced myself that if I could get through it with her, then she would learn to trust and I would become a more patient and understanding man.

twenty

MID-AUGUST

The compassion that Michelle had shown for the ill child gave me an idea. It was clear that Michelle did best when she did not feel threatened with abandonment or when there could be no doubt that the love she was receiving was unconditional. I asked her if she wanted a puppy and she glowed at the prospect. She spent the next few days scanning the newspapers. One evening I came home and found what appeared to be the rear end of a large fluffy orange rabbit growling under the bed. It darted after some unseen object and then reappeared as a dog a few moments later. Michelle laughed at the antics of the puppy, a three-month-old cocker spaniel. The dog had so much energy that he seemed to bounce rather than walk, but when he did walk he wagged his rear end with such force that he appeared to swagger like the bear in *The Jungle Book*. We named him Balu.

Balu quickly became attached to us, particularly to Michelle. The presence of the dog seemed to calm her, and for a while her fear that I would leave her seemed to fade. While I was at the hospital, Michelle would take Balu for walks and house-train him. But soon even the puppy was not able to keep her from thinking about her own emptiness. Again she grew restless and found grievance with the smallest frustration. She was becoming more depressed, and I felt more pressure to do something to relieve her of her misery.

One evening after work she told me that she had an idea. She told me that she wanted me to transfer to a hospital closer to home. The idea appealed to me too, not so much because I was unhappy with my job but more because I felt emotionally depleted. I needed help to deal with Michelle's intensity and unpredictability. Back home I was sure that she would once again be able to get herself a job. At least she would have her friends and family to visit with during the hours I was away.

The next morning I woke early and called the teaching hospitals back in Miami, but all the intern posts had been filled. Still, the idea of leaving had taken root in Michelle's head. She would not tolerate an entire year in the desert. "I guess I could commute back and forth. You know, go home, spend two weeks, and then come back for a week," she offered. Once again she was looking for a way to make the relationship work. She suggested a schedule of spending a week with me in Taos, alternating with—before her anticipated frustration with my work schedule set in—a week at home. "I spoke to my grandmother this morning. She told me that she would pay for the airplane tickets."

We agreed to test out her idea and bought her a ticket to go home. Immediately, Michelle seemed more at ease. The next day I drove her to the airport in Santa Fe and she left for Miami. I had thought that her leaving would be easy for me, but instead I found myself missing her desperately. Her emotional hold on me, and her companionship, were far more profound than I had expected. Without her being with me, I found that my feelings were strangely without context. My joys, sorrows, and fears had become subject to Michelle's state of mind. I could not generate feelings for their own sake without feeling guilty. She had only just left, yet I missed her.

Tears blurred my vision on the drive back to the apartment. The emotion was more complex than just sadness at her not being with me. There was also a contradictory feeling, a sense of being free and being able to breathe again. I took pleasure at the thought of calling my family, unencumbered by the possibility of discovery by Michelle and the resulting outburst. But then my fear that she would discover this betrayal, or even that I had thought of it, made me anxious. I pulled over to the side of the road and sat in the car for ten minutes trying to make sense of these feelings. I couldn't make sense of them, but the ten minutes had cleared my tears, and I made it home safely.

One evening the charge-nurse paged me to ask about a terminally ill patient. The situation was complex. His family wanted him to come home and did not want him to be on the intravenous morphine that was reducing his pain from cancer. We spent a long time discussing the options. Immediately after I hung up, the phone rang. It was Michelle.

"Hi, baby," I said excitedly. "What's going on? How are you doing?"

"Who were you speaking to?" she demanded. "As soon as I turn my back, you get on the phone with your family again." It was as if she had read my earlier thoughts. I felt guilty for this and then angry at feeling guilty.

"It was the ward. I was doing my work."

Quickly she became her sometimes-sweet self. "I'm sorry, baby, I just miss you terribly. I wanted to talk to you and hear your voice again. I'll be back soon." There was a yearning in her voice that appealed to me. I slept well that night.

A week later, I picked her up at the airport. "Babe, you are going to love me so much. I didn't sit around the last two weeks. I went to a hospital in Boca Raton. It's just over forty miles from my parents' home. I spoke to the medical director. God, I was good. I totally seduced him! He is going to offer you an internship for your remaining ten months. Isn't that great? They will have a position ready in two weeks. Time to start packing!"

One of the reasons I had chosen Taos was because I wanted to work in a community-based health service. I wanted to be in a small hospital, one where I could practice all of medicine, from dermatology to obstetrics, not isolating care to one specific organ of the body. This desire to do community medicine in a small town came into direct conflict with Michelle's needs. She needed the anonymity of a big city. "God, I don't want the neighbors to know our business and then spread it around. In a town like this everybody will know in days. How do you think that will make me feel?"

I had conflicting priorities and goals, but now she was my family. I didn't want her to be miserable because of something that could so easily be changed. I decided that she was right, so the next day I went to the hospital administration to explain my decision. The medical director said, "We are not surprised. The housing administrator called us when you requested a change in your living quarters. Good luck in Boca Raton. I think you'll need it." They seemed to understand, but I am sure that in that small community nothing got missed. Her tantrums had not been quiet.

Michelle was happy now, almost euphoric. She had our few belongings packed a week ahead of our departure. For her, my decision to go back to Miami was a new level of commitment. "Babe, thank you so much. No one would ever have done that for me before." She cooked every night and scrubbed the apartment clean every day, just to keep busy. She went out and bought Cadbury chocolate, which we ate by the slab while we watched videos.

"If we could choose to spend the rest of our lives doing this, I would make the choice right now," she said happily. During the next few days we had neither a fight nor a single cruel word between us. For those few days, I believed that she was beginning to believe in herself and to hold my love for her inside her mind. I believed that she was healing.

With two days to go before our departure, I told Michelle that I was going to call my parents to let them know what we were up to. Michelle's mood shifted rapidly. She became suddenly irritable and then just as suddenly calm. After a brief phone call letting my parents know of our plans, we went to wash a last load of laundry when my pager went off. I had to return to the ward to evaluate a patient who had made a sudden turn for the worse. Michelle started screaming.

"What are you doing to me? Just because you think I'm better doesn't mean that you can act as if I'm normal. Just because we're going home doesn't mean that you can call or see your parents whenever you want to."

I had to get to the ward. "Don't walk away. Listen to me!" she shrieked. She ran up to me, grabbed my pager, and threw it to the floor. It smashed open.

"What the hell are you doing? We are going to have to pay for that thing. You're an idiot."

I surprised myself. It was the first time that I had ever insulted her. She picked up a pair of scissors and pointed them at me. I moved to take them away from her.

"Take another step and I will squeeze your balls so hard that you'll never come again," she threatened. The thought of this made me shudder, but foolishly I dared her to try.

"You wouldn't."

With scissors in one hand she moved in quickly, grabbed my groin, and started to squeeze. I grabbed her hand and pulled it away but the damage was done and the pain came quickly. I dropped to the ground. She continued to come after me with the pair of scissors.

In a moment of self-preservation I grabbed a framed oil painting that she had been working on for her mother and held it up as she lunged. The scissors tore through the canvas easily. She was stunned momentarily as she realized the damage done to her painting. Taking the opportunity of her inaction and still angry with her, I took the scissors and began cutting up the canvas, completely destroying it.

She ran at me, but now I was calmer, more aware. Maybe this was the same calm that she felt after her outbursts. I turned and picked her up, carried her to the bedroom, and dumped her on the bed. She laughed, which surprised me, and she sat up suddenly and grabbed my shirt, tearing it open. "God that turned me on, I want you to fuck me now!" The anger had turned to desire, but so it was with Michelle, and that in part was why I loved her. Just like a drug, she had a way of making

95

me feel ecstatic, but also like with a drug, there were many lows. I would crash and then need her to pick me up again.

Later I tried to piece my pager together. The paging mechanism had not been damaged and the case held together well with tape. After returning the pager to the office, I drove slowly back to the apartment. Our time in the desert was done. The car packed, we started the long drive back home as the evening sun bade its farewell in brown, red, orange, and blue, and the town settled back for a restful night.

twenty-one

EARLY SEPTEMBER
BOCA RATON, FLORIDA

The drive back to Florida was fairly uneventful. On the second day of driving, after a long stretch of silence, Michelle told me that she had lined up a few job interviews for herself, having recognized that she had to have something to do during the day. When I told her I thought that it was a good idea that she get a job, she became angry, saying, "Why is it a good idea? So you can get rid of me? So you don't have to worry about me? Well, let me tell you that if that's the way you feel, maybe I won't go." This time her attempt to rile me was unsuccessful. I didn't respond to her outburst with a no-win answer. Neither, "Yes, so that I can get rid of you," nor, "No, it's because I think that a job will help your self-esteem," would have been the right answer. She seemed genuinely happy with my lack of response as we continued on our way.

After a weekend at her parents' house, we drove to my new hospital in Boca Raton. An infinitely more manageable city than Miami, Boca Raton lies to the south of Palm Beach about forty-five miles north of Miami, and all three are connected conveniently by I-95.

Unlike in Taos, the medical center in Boca Raton was far

more fully integrated with the local medical school and bore all the trademarks of an academic establishment, with grand carvings of the great pioneers in medicine adorning its entrance hall. Like in Taos, the hospital in Boca Raton provided some inexpensive and characterless housing. After reviewing the limited choices, we settled on a corner condominium with views of the Atlantic and a grove of palm trees, both of which punctuated the difference between our last two months and our current setting. The apartment block housed only doctors and nurses, and unlike in Taos, marital status was never considered in the allocation of units.

The next day, Michelle headed back for her interviews in Miami, and I met with the administrative secretary for a schedule of my assignments. The first rotation would be a two-month stint on a pediatric in-patient unit. The call schedule was one night on call every three. "You won't get any sleep when you are on call," warned the friendly assistant. "The kids are very sick, but the staff knows their stuff. You can trust them." After my first night on call, I knew that she was right. The hospital in Taos had been humane in its call demands, and there had always been time for a few hours of sleep. Now the expectations were higher, the problems more complex, and the chief residents more demanding. Michelle decided to stay at her parents' house for my nights on call. "I can't get any sleep anyway. You get paged too much."

On the days I was on call I would get to work by seven in the morning and not get home until six in the evening the next day. When I wasn't on call it was a straight eleven-hour day. There was no time to exercise, and Michelle spent her early evenings after work cooking lavish, butter-heavy comfort meals or finding restaurants that would do the same. In the seven months that I had known her I had put on close to forty pounds. "You are eating so much because you are miserable," my mother told me one day. "It's a substitute for love." I couldn't think about whether she was right. The idea that I was substituting food for love was more than I could handle during the brutality of the work schedule.

I looked forward to being with Michelle in the evenings, and she seemed happy with her new job. She had finally accepted a position at a beauty counter in a large department store. The job worked out well for her because she did not need to be in until after ten in the morning and could leave by three. The schedule gave her a good chance to succeed because she liked to sleep late in the mornings and then be at home when I returned from the hospital.

Michelle had not been able to keep her previous jobs for any significant period of time. She told me that she had had problems with her bosses, with her coworkers, or with the work schedule. "I couldn't stand how utterly boring my jobs were. Believe me, I tried. Eventually I just told them to get fucked, or I didn't show up, and then I told my mother to call them and say that I had quit." This cosmetics job was different. Her pay was based mainly on commissions, so she did well.

There were times when she was so angry that all I could see was the ugliness of her character and I couldn't bear spending time with her. But most of the time this was not the case with Michelle. Partly it was because she was beautiful. No other word would do her justice. She was not cute, or gorgeous, or stunning, or dazzling, or elegant. And even when I was angry with her, her beauty overcame me. It did her a disservice in a way because it hid the pain and the fear and the emptiness. In some sense she was like a mirage, an empty promise that teases with hope but is ultimately barren when you approach it for consistent substance. But she was beautiful, and so she sold cosmetics magnificently.

A few weeks after the start of my new position, Michelle had another idea. "Why is it that I have to drive over an hour in heavy traffic to get to work and then drive another hour back to this apartment only to sit around and wait for you? I think that we should move back to my parents' home for the nights that you are not on call and then at least when I get home, my brother or my parents will be there or I could meet up with a friend. My mother would cook all the meals and she would do the laundry. On the nights that you are on call you could stay at the apartment here."

"We have to give Boca Raton some time. We just got here," I protested feebly. I did not have the will to fight her on this, and some of what she said appealed to me. "Can we agree to talk about it again after we have tried to settle here?" I asked unconvincingly. I was at the point of complete breakdown now. By being with Michelle I had lost control of my emotions and my weight. Now, if we moved back to Miami, I would lose control of my autonomy and, increasingly, or so I felt, of my life. But Michelle was getting closer to the shelter of being in a familiar and predictable environment. I felt that it was only a matter of time until the subject of moving to her parents' house came up again. I knew that when that happened I would lose that battle too.

Work was demanding. The first two months were spent on the pediatric surgical floor. I was happy to end the rotation. I was sure that I didn't want to specialize in pediatric surgery after seeing the heartbroken families with their devastated young children with kidney cancers and blocked bowels. The doctors doing this work were surely answering a much higher calling. I checked my schedule. Obstetrics and gynecology was next, and I told Michelle so one evening.

"God, I hope that you wash yourself well before you touch me with those smelly fingers. Aren't you disgusted with yourself, spending your days telling women to spread their legs and looking up their vaginas? Why can't you get a real job like a real man? I am sure that there are plenty of men that appreciate my body. How would you like it if I invited men over and started feeling their balls?"

The tension was back, and again it worsened with the demands of my rigorous on-call schedule and nights away from home. For me, though, the nights that I was called in were a reprieve. They provided a sleepless calm before the certain storm of the next day.

One night my pager went off during supper. A young woman had arrived by ambulance in early labor and was experiencing some bleeding.

"Shit, man!" shouted Michelle. "There you go again! Why the fuck should I stay here if you are never going to be home?"

"But it's the work that I do," I protested.

"Bullshit, you asshole. It's what you have chosen to do. It is a choice to not be with me. I could be with another man, and maybe that's what you need. A little competition to keep you interested. So many men want me and you know it. Maybe I should be with somebody who works a real job. Somebody who doesn't think that work is more important than me. Anyway, these days you're so exhausted it's like you've forgotten how to fuck. We used to go four times a night, and now your pathetic thing gives me no pleasure. Fuck me like a real man, or I'll find someone who will."

Michelle reliably resorted to the threat to be with another man whenever she felt that I wasn't paying her enough attention. Predictably, I felt threatened, and she knew it. It was her way of making me feel inadequate and it worked. My mother once told me, "If you want your wife to love you, then you have to be a provider and a protector. Even if you love her, without protecting and providing for her and her children, she will never respect you." I had taken this wisdom to heart, but with Michelle I felt I was failing in my mission to be a good husband. That sense of failure was intolerable, so I lashed out. "If you do that, I'll leave you," I threatened. "No wonder men have always left you. You make life impossible for them," I said vengefully.

"But you know that about me. You promised me better. You promised never to leave me."

I felt guilty for having retaliated. I was caught in the trap of hating her for the very weaknesses that had drawn me to her. But worse, I had promised her that I would love her despite her insecurities and rage. By promising that I would never leave her, I had guaranteed her unconditional love. She continued to put this promise to the test.

"We both knew that this was going to be a difficult year," I said defensively.

"Damn you. What about me? Who is going to take care of me?" she cried.

"I am your husband, not your therapist. And I do take care of you. I spend every waking second that I am not at the hospital with you."

I turned to look for my white coat, and then heard a loud pathetic scream, almost a screech, behind me. I turned to face her and she lashed out, striking me in the face. I covered my face while she continued her attack, kicking and hitting. Finally, I grabbed her arms and held her in a bear hug. She continued to scream, "Help, *help*, he's trying to kill me." Foolishly, I tried to put my hand across her mouth, but she bit hard into my palm. I heard the neighbors at the door, and eventually the landlord opened it.

"Please," I asked, "call an ambulance. My wife isn't well." They didn't appear convinced, so I let her go.

"You fucking call an ambulance and I'll kill myself now, I swear it," she threatened, grabbing a kitchen knife. Someone asked me if they should call the police but I assured them that we had gone through this before and that I could handle it. My pager went off. "Dr. Walker, you are needed in the delivery room right away!"

"Okay, darling, we won't call an ambulance, but I have to get to the delivery room. I want you to relax, watch TV, and I'll be back as soon as I'm done." One of the neighbors, a nurse, offered to spend the evening with Michelle.

"I just can't take it anymore," said Michelle. She started to cry and put the knife down. "Go, I'll take something to calm me down. I'm just going to sleep tonight."

The next morning she woke me early and we lay in bed, talking. "Babe, I know that we just moved here from Taos, but even being this close to Miami isn't helping. I just can't take it being here all alone with nothing to do. I just go crazy looking at the walls."

"What would help? You could read, watch TV, or paint or get a full-time job or do some housework. Your mom said that I should get you to do housework."

"If only we could live at my parents' house. You promised that we would talk about it again, remember? If only we could leave Boca Raton, everything would be perfect. I could talk to my mom and my friends when you're away, and I promise you I would look to get a full-time job. You could still keep the apartment for whenever you are on call. At least I wouldn't get so lonely. It drives me crazy. I'm sorry for what I did last night." She smiled warmly. "I love you so much, you're so good to me. I know that things will work out." Slowly she removed the T-shirt I had worn to bed and gently kissed my chest. "And I'm sorry about all the things I said last night. You're my best lover ever, it's just that I miss you."

I felt more relaxed. "Okay, if you find yourself a full-time job, I'll agree to move back. But you must find a job." Michelle increased her work schedule from four hours to six hours a day, and I kept my end of the deal and agreed to make her parents' house our base. I resigned myself to the forty-five-mile commute to work every day.

twenty-two

MID-NOVEMBER

Even though I had spoken to my parents periodically since my marriage to Michelle, I had not seen them in more than four months. But now Michelle seemed increasingly more convinced that I would not abandon her. One morning I suggested having lunch with my parents. At first she appeared irritated with the idea, but later that evening, after a session with her therapist, she agreed to the plan without further fuss. I was heartened by her reaction. She hated how close I was to my family, so I felt that she was giving something back to me. What had bothered me most about not seeing them was not the absence of seeing them only, but that I had become terrified of even suggesting it to Michelle for fear that she would erupt in anger. Her agreeing to meet with my parents was a breakthrough. She agreed to lunch as long as it was on neutral ground. We settled on a restaurant at a nearby country club.

As the weekend approached, Michelle became more irritable and demanding. I did everything I could to make sure that things would work out. On Thursday she said, "Look, I don't want to go. They are your parents. You go. You haven't seen them in a long time." I recognized the trap immediately.

"Darling, you know that I want you to be there with me.

105

You are doing so well. I want you to be there for them to see how happy you make me. You are my wife." She seemed appeased by my words and I hoped she would believe and hold on to them for at least the next two days. If Michelle could now believe that I could care for her at the same time that I could care for another, or that by caring for somebody else it was not taking away from my care for her, then she had truly made progress.

I had ordered my parents to be on their best behavior, and they reassured me that this was to be a dinner of conciliation. They promised that it would be the first step on the return to normality. I was happy, but it seemed to me that happiness was no longer an emotion that I could feel for its own sake. I had to justify everything to myself. "I am happy because . . . I am sad because . . . I am angry because . . ." The natural ebb and flow of feeling from within, without apparent cause, was gone. Sometimes when I felt happy I felt guilty for feeling what Michelle felt so rarely.

My father called that Saturday morning to say that the country club required a coat and tie. I wanted my father to know that I appreciated the effort that he was making, so I chose a tie that he had given me some time back.

"What's that?" asked Michelle, pointing to the tie. I tensed, anxious, wary of her question.

"It's a tie. My dad gave it to me once."

"Well, take it off; it's ugly."

I had to hold firm. "Come on, Michelle, it's a peace offering. I'm going to wear it. It's no big deal. Why don't you just get ready and we'll go? They're waiting for us."

"You just can't let go of them, can you?" Her voice was rising.

"Listen, this is your parents' house that we're living in. I haven't seen mine in months. I am not the one who can't let go."

"Yes, but I *need* my parents. I need to see them and feel them and be near them. God, I know that you know that. I know what you are trying to do to me. Don't compare my situation to yours."

"Okay, let's just relax and go," I said softly.

"Take that fucking tie off!" she demanded.

"This tie is not an issue. Let's go."

"The tie is ugly and it shows your father's bad taste."

I turned to the mirror one last time in order to straighten the tie out. "Here, let me help you with it," she said. I turned, confused, as she grabbed the tie and with the slice of a pair of scissors, cut it in half. "Now you can take it off. That should make it easier," she said calmly. "Let's go. You can borrow one of my dad's."

A sense of utter disbelief, rage, and violation overwhelmed me. I sat on the bed with clenched fists and cried for the loss of the tie. I wanted her to feel the hurt that I felt, but even worse, at that moment I wanted to be the one hurting her. The thought of hurting her was sobering. "She is sick, she is sick, she is sick . . ." I repeated over and over. I swallowed, as if by doing so I could move the anger to the pit of my stomach. Eventually I stood up. "Okay, let's go now."

"I am not ready yet," she said.

"Bye, I'm leaving."

Her parents had heard the commotion and were hovering outside the bedroom. They saw the anger in my face as I left the room. "What happened?" I threw down the cut tie and headed for the car. Michelle came running after me. I slammed the car door shut. "Okay, okay, but give me just a minute," she insisted. She tapped on the car window, lips offering a conciliatory kiss. I lowered the window and she leant into the car to kiss me. "Sorry, sorry, sorry." Immediately she grabbed the keys out of the ignition. "I told you to wait until I was ready. Are you fucking deaf? You weren't going to leave without me, were you?" She headed for the house, and I ran after her. Her mother stopped me and handed me her car keys. "Here, take my car. Just go."

I got into the car and left. Free at last. I headed for the gate. Behind me, I heard the unmistakable sound of the Mustang revving. Michelle's mother's car was a slow, low-powered excuse of a car. Quickly, Michelle caught up to me and overtook me. I cringed at the thought of the action on the narrow, suburban, potentially child-filled street. Suddenly she braked, and I swerved off the road to avoid hitting her. I drove around her, as she had stalled, but again she caught up and I turned down another street to get away.

Her mother's car was no match, and it was crazy driving around like this. Defeated, I returned to the house. We were already an hour late for lunch; meanwhile, she decided to continue driving around the block. Faster and faster and faster she drove, but even worse, in a low gear. The sound was the terrifying grind of an over-revved engine. Her parents stood there watching, feeling as hopeless and lost as I was. I prayed that a child wouldn't run out. I heard a crash and then more screeching.

Michelle's brother called to me. "Your mother is on the phone." I told her of the nightmare. She said that she understood and that she wanted to pray for us, but I felt too empty for prayers. I heard my car coming down the driveway. There was a dent in the front fender. Michelle looked exhausted. "I crashed into a rock," she admitted.

It was at this moment that I realized that I might not be able to keep my promise to be with her for the rest of my life. Previously, the thought had crossed my mind but had left quickly. Now I considered it for more than just a moment, and found some solace in the thought.

I had been committed to the belief that my love for her would cure her. Now I looked at her, as miserable as she was, and I could not conjure up this thought anymore, in part because I was having difficulty conjuring up love for her right then. I was having difficulty conjuring up love or self-respect for myself. Is this what it had to come to, my becoming her, assuming her personality? Could either of us be saved? I had believed that giving her what she had never had—strong, unrelenting, and unconditional love—would fill the emptiness and uncertainties she felt. But it was never enough, and moreover it had emptied me out, so there were now two of us empty of feeling and hungry for love.

How much would she test me? "No one could ever love me forever," she had said so many times. Maybe she would prove this to be true. She kept upping her demands of me; slowly destroying whatever hope I had to show her that she was lovable. I wasn't sure that I could keep up with her unrelenting neediness.

Was it so terrifying to be loved, or was the thought of losing such love even more terrifying? I didn't know what the answer was, and I seriously doubted that I would ever find out. I was empty and could no longer feel; I had nothing left to give.

I couldn't understand it. Short of transplanting myself into her body, what would it ever take for her to hold me inside of her? She told me that she felt the feeling when we made love, but that the further I moved away from her the duller the feeling became. I felt that I had given everything I could, and the paradox became clear to me then: The more I gave, the more she wanted because I could never quite give enough. There was always that little bit more. In order to give more I would have to be strong. Yet the more I gave, the more pathetic and weak I became. It could never work.

twenty-three

Michelle was uncharacteristically subdued after the car scene. She poured her remaining energy into her work at the cosmetics counter. We moved quietly through the days, not mentioning the event, as if not talking about it would make it disappear, make it never have existed. It would be her birthday in six weeks and I wanted to make it a memorable day.

Michelle could not believe that people loved her, or at least she found it hard to believe it when they were not physically with her, reassuring her of the fact. Without the person being in her presence, any feeling of the permanence of love seemed to disappear. It seemed normal to me to be thinking about her a lot of the time. Planning for her birthday was an act of love— not an unusual act of love, but one that goes unseen. Thinking about where we would go and what we would do was not like a dozen roses that she could hold and smell, but it was thinking about her and what would make her happy. Increasingly I realized that these unseen acts of love meant nothing to her. She could not internalize them because they weren't tangible. It was as if they never happened. Had I not planned for her birthday, however, or had I forgotten it altogether, she would have seen this as proof that I didn't love her.

On the day of her birthday, I left the hospital early and

stopped to pick up a bunch of peonies. As I got back in the car, my voice-activated beeper went off: "Dr. Walker, call Ward Three immediately." The voice sounded urgent, and I stopped at a pay phone. The charge nurse answered. "Mr. Smith, in bed six, has had a sudden rise in temperature. He has a fever of 104. He looks terrible." A sudden dread fell over me. I hated Mr. Smith. He was doing this on purpose. Surely I would arrive late for Michelle, and she would believe that I had done it on purpose. "You don't love me more than anything," she would say. But Mr. Smith was dying. I certainly had to take care of him.

I drove back quickly. A fellow intern was still at the hospital. She told me that she was on call that night and that I should order all the tests I wanted. She would take over the case after that and review the results. I checked to see that Mr. Smith was comfortable and not in any clear emergency. I ordered some X rays and blood work. Some Tylenol and a cool glass of water lowered his temperature. I reassured him that he would be okay and that I was leaving him in the capable hands of my colleague. He smiled back at me through thin lips. "Thank you."

I drove back home, too fast, but I was already late. I thought of the past six weeks and reminded myself that she had done well. Moreover, there was nothing I could do. I was in peak rush-hour traffic.

I arrived home at 6:15. Michelle was waiting in the driveway.

"Where the fuck have you been?" she demanded, grabbing the peonies out of my hands and throwing them angrily to the ground. "Why are you late? Who the fuck were you with? Were you with some little nurse? You couldn't make it here on time?"

Michelle had an unparalleled ability to conjure up the most unlikely events imaginable. She would work herself up into a state of frenzy, paranoid that I was being disloyal or creating scenarios that had no basis in reality. And when she did so, these imaginings became her reality. It was one thing to fear her rage for something that I had actually done, but it was the fear of her anger at her created fantasies that terrified me the most. I had no defense.

"If you flip out, you can forget about tonight," I threatened her.

She screamed loud and long and came toward me. I thought of the scissors that she had previously used on my tie, and made the decision to run around the back of the house, heading for the pool. She ran back into the house and her mother tried to console her.

"He's back. I told you he'd be back. You married a doctor. Just go out and have a nice dinner."

"He could have tried harder," she cried. "He could have tried harder." She came out again. "Anthony, come here!"

"Not until you calm down."

She went back into the house and picked up a potted plant, then hurled it at the living room wall. She picked up another and threw it through a small window, then another one at the Chagall-like flower arrangement that she had painted for me. She sat down and sobbed inconsolably into her hands. "He could have tried harder."

I came to her and put my arm around her shoulders. She buried her face in my neck and her body relaxed. Finally, with the anger gone, we were able to enjoy dinner at her favorite Italian restaurant.

I had a nightmare that night. Michelle's mother was teaching a cooking class. A pot on the stove had started to boil over. She wasn't strong enough to hold the lid down and asked me to take over. I held it down as tightly as I could, but eventually could hold it no longer. The pot erupted, scalding me. She thanked me for holding the lid, but the water had spilled over so she would have to add more. She asked me to hold the lid down again.

twenty-four

Early on in the relationship, Michelle had asked me to promise her that I would never hit her. It seemed a strange request, but she told me that all of her previous boyfriends had hit her at some point in their relationship with her. I could never imagine myself hitting her, or anyone else for that matter. I promised her that I would never hit her.

Our relationship was physical though, in love and in anger. When Michelle was angry she threw, punched, bit, scratched, and kicked. In turn I would dodge, block, and run. Occasionally I would wrestle with her to hold her. Her arms would flail and she would yell as she attempted to scratch me. The time I tried to put my hand across her mouth and she bit it, I ended up with stitches and a tetanus booster.

One evening I arrived home exhausted and headed straight for bed, then quickly fell asleep. The previous night I had had no sleep after being on call. Soon, though, I felt Michelle shaking me.

"I told you never to bring your work home. When you get home your time is my time."

Too tired to argue, I fell back asleep.

"Get the fuck up, you miserable prick!" she shrieked.

I jumped up with frazzled nerves. In her hand she had a pair of scissors.

"This should wake you up!"

I fell back on the bed and grabbed her hand. And then I slapped her.

Michelle stopped, stunned. "You promised me." She held her hand to her face. I was awake then.

"I'm sorry, I'm sorry, I'm sorry." I held her. "I promise you that I will never do that again." For the briefest of moments it had felt good to hurt her, and then instantly everything was wrong. I started to cry. I had lost complete control of everything I believed in. The nausea of my act overwhelmed me.

"You promised."

"I'm sorry," I sobbed.

"I can never trust you again. I can never believe your promises. You aren't any better than any of the others. My mother was wrong. You aren't my guardian angel." She looked at her face in the mirror. Her cheek was red and swollen, the pain magnified by her tears. Her face had drawn me to her. My promise of enduring love and care had drawn her to me. Both were now damaged, though her face would heal quicker. She used makeup to hide the mark on her face.

Now, at home she trailed me like a chastened puppy. I was angry at my loss of control. It took another month before she argued with me again; it was an eerie and uncomfortable time.

twenty-five

Michelle was now seeing her therapist every other week. They would spend the hour-and-a-half working on strategies to control her rage.

"I am all these pieces all at once," Michelle once told me, "and I can't hold them all together. I keep falling apart. Don't you see why it would be better for me to be dead than to live this way? I wish that you could be inside me to hold me together. That's why I get so frightened when you leave me."

I was finding it increasingly difficult to have the strength necessary to deal with her unpredictable moods and raging behavior. At one point her therapist referred her to a psychiatrist. "In some centers they are trying antipsychotic medication and mood stabilizers for this condition. I haven't had much luck with these medications, but we can try," he told her. I was not sure how medication would change her personality, but Michelle agreed to try. First, she took Mellaril, which the psychiatrist said would help her think more clearly. "It hasn't done anything for my thinking," Michelle later said. "Obviously because there is nothing wrong with my thinking, but it helps me sleep better." She also tried Tegretol to control her moods, but she felt that it didn't work so she stopped taking it. She took a dose of Valium once, but it made her feel more rageful. "God,

I never want to feel like that again," she said, after she had calmed down some hours later.

Intellectually I felt that I understood her illness better, but I had a hard time separating what was illness from what sometimes looked like willful and vengeful behavior. She blamed everything that went wrong on her condition, or on me. Maybe I could have understood this better, but I was her husband and not her therapist. I had a hard time remembering that sometimes.

The course of my every day was set by her moods. I had no control over this. If she was happy, I felt calm. When she was angry, I was edgy all day, unable to focus at work. I wondered if this chaos was what she felt inside. It was unbearable for both of us. I was beginning to understand her, but it was draining me.

After we had returned from Taos and were back in Miami, I tried to reconnect with some of my old classmates. They returned the calls, but Michelle never gave me the messages.

"I wonder why they aren't calling back?" I asked her.

"Don't worry, babe. You don't need them. You've got me."

Once, Howard called and I answered.

"Hey, brother, I've been trying to get a hold of you for the last few months. I guess you're a busy man, even too busy for your friends," he laughed.

"What are you talking about? I had no idea."

"Didn't Michelle tell you I had called?"

"No, she said nothing."

Later I confronted her on this. "Why didn't you tell me that Howard had called?"

She erupted into rage. "What the fuck do you need any of

your friends for now? You've got me. What do you want to talk to them about that you can't say to me? Soon you'll want to go out for a drink with them and leave me here by myself, but I tell you the minute you try that I'll be fucking another man."

There was no middle ground for her. It was always all or nothing. Later that week I called Howard from the hospital and we agreed to a secret meeting for lunch at the hospital cafeteria. My stomach pitted with anxiety, fearing that she would find out. When she was in one of her moments of madness, there was nothing to do. I realized that trying to talk to her or "do something" did little to calm the rage. In the big picture of her life, just my being there helped her more than anything else. I didn't know how to get out of the moments. They sucked me in each time and then spat me out. Each time I had less confidence in myself.

Howard drove up from Miami. His internship, like mine, was half-complete. Unlike mine, he had spent the entire time at one hospital, Miami General. "God, Howard, in the last six months I have worked in two hospitals while living in three cities in two states."

"You're not yourself. You've lost your spark," he told me. "I wish we'd understood more about borderlines last year. She didn't look that bad. You were thinking with the wrong head." I laughed with him, but the laughter brought me no joy.

"Thanks for coming. I wish I could see you all the time, but she feels so threatened by anyone I get close to."

"There is a Jewish teaching that goes like this: 'The way of the righteous and men of good deeds is to love peace and take pleasure in the welfare of their fellow-man and draw them closer to the Torah. They would not wantonly destroy even a mustard seed. They are grieved and oppressed at the sight of waste and destruction. If they could save anything from being destroyed they would do so with all their power.'"

He paused, and then added, "You are a good man. You'll find the way. Call me whenever you want to," he offered. Then he continued with mischievous eyes, "Remember, you promised me that you were going to go into psychiatry to help children. If you're not careful, the only psychiatry you'll be seeing will be on my therapy couch."

twenty-six

JANUARY 1986

I woke up one morning feeling more miserable than usual. My clothes did not fit well. The bathroom scale read 220 pounds. I stood in front of the mirror and looked at the roll of fat that hung over my pants. "You're hideous," I told the reflection. I felt both lonely and alone. Everything annoyed me. During hospital rounds I compared my misery to the suffering of the patients I was treating. I felt that I needed to do that in order to not feel so bad.

If we were going to stay together, I had to change my role in the relationship. I felt that it had to be more on my terms. I had given up my life to prove my love to her. But it seemed to me that all my efforts had not been enough to make her feel more secure. I had to begin to distance myself from Michelle and become stronger. My mood could not be dependent upon how her day was going. I had to stop shying away from her aggression. I felt that her support systems—her family, her therapist, and her friends—enabled her dysfunction. This was not deliberate, but they provided her an outlet for her rage without forcing her to face her fears. They didn't challenge her to change because, like me, they treated her delicately for fear of unleashing a rageful monster.

I had to move her away from these supports. I had to force her to realize that she could survive without them. With this new sense of conviction, I made the decision to apply for a residency post anywhere but Miami. It had to be far enough for her to not easily escape from her fears by going back home, and it had to be a large enough city to offer ample employment and recreational opportunity as well as experienced psychotherapists. I was certain that leaving Miami had to be the first step in restoring control of my life—and of providing Michelle with any hope of breaking the cycle of despair that her life was.

I was finally beginning to face the truth of my situation.

I was determined to study psychiatry, and I knew that I would get no better training than in one of the East Coast programs. It was at this time that my deceit began. I sent for applications to nine different residency programs and used my father's home as the return address. When the packages arrived, my father paged me at the hospital. I picked them up at his house and took them to the hospital, where I left them in a locker for fear that Michelle would discover them at the apartment. One weekend my on-call duty began on Saturday morning and ended Sunday at noon. Michelle spent the weekend in Miami. After uneventful Saturday morning rounds, I retrieved the applications from the locker. I sat down at the nurses' station and opened the first package.

> Make sure to complete all sections as any omissions may lead to delays in processing your application. Please return the following with your 12-page application:
> —A letter from the office of the dean
> —Three letters of recommendation from supervisors

—A transcript of your medical school grades

—A resume

—Four passport-sized photos with your signature on
the back

—A half-page essay telling us why you want to come
to our training program

—A cashier's check for $120 (processing fee—do
not send cash or foreign currency)

The list continued. I feared that the chance of discovery
with all the application requirements was great. There were so
many elements. What if a secretary called the house and told
Michelle that my recommendation was ready? I would tell her
that I needed letters of recommendation for my local residency
applications. I wondered how I would get away in order to have
the passport-sized photographs taken. My father told me that
he would take care of the cashier's checks. I could not risk
having any mail inadvertently sent to our Boca Raton apartment or to Michelle's parents' house in Miami.

When I reviewed all the packages I found that much of the
requisite paperwork was similar for all the applications. That
meant just one trip to the photographer, one call to the dean's
office, and one call to each of three supervisors. Again I used
my parents' home as a return address and their phone number
as the contact number. Over the next few weeks I completed
the applications, a page at a time, during breaks at work. By
then the letters and transcripts had arrived. Again I lied to
Michelle and told her that my new rotation started half an hour
early. I used the extra time to meet with my father at the hospital and gave him the completed packages, which he then

mailed off. Six weeks later, all the applications had been sent.

Those days with Michelle were oddly peaceful. I did little to antagonize her, or at least she did not seem to be as easily bothered by the things I did. Perhaps I was extra sensitive to the fear of her discovering my subterfuge. Perhaps unconsciously I had already given up on her and did not feel that I had to challenge her any longer. In any case, Michelle was happy, and she was doing well at work. She seemed to be doing better. She laughed more easily and even made jokes, which was something new for her.

One evening we went out for dinner at a Portuguese restaurant. While waiting for our clams stewed in beer, an irate customer at the next table was shouting at the waitress that he had been waiting for his draft beer for some time. "If he wants a draft, why doesn't he shut up and go sit by that open window?" Michelle quipped. I laughed, not only for the joke, but also for how unexpected it was coming from her.

Her happiness had come at the expense of my own pathetic existence. But seeing her this happy made me not feel as sorry for myself as I had been feeling. To my surprise, one afternoon I arrived home to see her in a new jogging outfit. "It's Kappa. So are the running shoes. If we are going to go jogging, at least we should do it in style. You know me. Anyway, I think that we should jog every day. We could both use it."

Early on in our relationship, Michelle's unpredictability had been charming, with her intensity in her search for her identity, her spontaneous and unconventional lovemaking, and her energy in creating art. But this did not last long, and increasingly the only unpredictability was just when the next tantrum would occur. Her sudden decision to go jogging was unexpected and refreshing.

"I agree. What made you think of it?"

"I know how much you like to run. Anyway, I read in my *Cosmo* that running at least thirty minutes four times a week means that you increase your metabolism by burning off an extra two thousand calories. We could both use that. My mother said that she would come too."

"Michelle, you're doing great. You're joking around, you want to start exercising, you seem so much happier. What is it?"

"You're just not provoking me like you used to. Also, you don't talk about your parents so much. Maybe we'll even be able to visit them soon," she said, as if she were granting me a favor.

A few weeks later my father called me. I had received responses to my applications. All were positive. All had appointment dates and interviews set up. I was living two lives, but in my secret I had regained some control. I felt sad for Michelle, knowing that I would have to tell her soon, knowing the disappointment and betrayal that she would feel. But the worst was knowing that the abandonment that she had predicted, that is, my abandonment of her, would come at a time when her belief in herself was apparently just starting to take root.

"In the end, everybody leaves me."

twenty-seven

MID-FEBRUARY

Nearly three months went by without Michelle having a major incident, with only occasional displays of rapidly ending irritation. There was no throwing, no hitting, no biting, no rage attacks, and most notably no suicide threats. One weekend her parents left for vacation, and like adolescents we took over the house and organized a party for each night.

Friday night started with far too much Merlot and continued with total loss of inhibitions. We danced naked in the pool and fumbled in love in the kitchen. Eventually exhaustion set in, and we fell asleep at some late hour. Some time after that the ringing in my head started, and I got up for a drink of water and then went back to bed. The ringing started again, and then stopped. It started again. It took a while for me to realize that it wasn't coming from my head. The telephone persisted. "Leave it," muttered Michelle. It rang again. Now it began to scare me the way a late-night call does.

"Hello?"

"Anthony, it's your brother Michael."

"Hey, what's up? Do you know what time it is?"

"Anthony, I have terrible news. Ryan called. Rachel has been killed in a car accident."

"What are you talking about?"

"Ryan was driving behind them. He saw everything. He said that Rachel was sitting on the passenger side of the car in front of him. She was on the way back home after being at church with her friends. Some drunken guy drove through a stop sign and into her side of the car. She died instantly."

I hung up and felt cold. I loved my sister, but I had rarely told her how much she meant to me. I had never been a good older brother, often outwardly dismissive of her achievements. In truth, I secretly admired her successes. She was the first in the family to graduate with a college degree, the first to own her own car, the first to pay off her college loans, the first to become financially independent of my parents. We teased and ribbed her, but she smiled, and when I needed a summer job she offered me hers. "I've got connections; I'll just get another." She was selfless. She had been killed by the selfishness of a man who drank and then drove. He too had been killed in the accident. But even in his death I hated him for having taken her.

"My sister just died in a car accident."

It took moments of tragedy to bring out the sympathy that Michelle was capable of feeling and showing. I remembered how she had cared for the little boy with the enlarged brain in the hospital in Taos. Now she put her arm around me and said simply, "Babe, I'm sorry." I cried and continued to cry, and at some point fell back asleep.

During my time with Michelle I had spent little time with my parents, but I had spent even less time with Rachel. Because of this, to Michelle, Rachel was the least threatening of my family members. They had met on two occasions. The first time was soon after Michelle and I had started dating. Rachel was preparing to move to San Francisco to attend graduate school, so the meeting was brief. The second time that she met Michelle was when Rachel came to Miami during a school vacation and had lunch with us. It was also the last time I would ever see Rachel or speak to her. She told me that she was on track for a master's degree in psychology. I remember being impressed by how Rachel once again had a clear vision of her life's course.

Always kind, always gentle, and always generous, Rachel told me after lunch, "Anthony, that is what is so great about you. You give hope to people who are miserable. Mom told me about Michelle. She seems so happy. If anybody can help her, you can." And that was it; she saw the good in people all the time. My brother Ryan, who had been with her when she died, told me that she prayed for me daily that God would give me the strength to help Michelle.

Early the next morning I woke from the nightmare, although I have never experienced such a vivid nightmare. Michael's voice had seemed real. Had he called? "Hi, Mom," I called my mother. She was crying. I remember somebody once telling me that a child who loses a parent is called an orphan but that there is no word for a parent who loses a child. It is unnatural. I could not imagine how much my mother was hurting. Rachel was her first daughter.

Some days after Rachel's death, my mother told me that Rachel's spirit had visited her in the form of a songbird. The bird had told my mother that she was happy to have finally made it to heaven.

My father made the funeral arrangements. In a moment of sudden, raw bitterness toward Michelle, I wanted her to try to stop me from going to the funeral by having one of her tantrums. I wanted to get angry at her and yell at her for her insensitivity, and for having kept me from my family. Michelle never gave me the opportunity; she was kind and solemn throughout. The hurt did not come from Michelle, but from her mother. "Your poor mother," she said. "But at least it's not as bad as losing your only daughter. At least she has two others. That's why some people have a lot of children." I lost total respect for Michelle's mother after she made that admission. I felt that this lack of caring had, in part, made Michelle the person she was. How could Michelle ever believe that anybody cared for her when her mother was so incapable of understanding the loss of a child? How could she not understand the uniqueness of every child's relationship with his or her parents?

Michelle and I flew to Los Angeles for the funeral. Rachel was buried on a mountainside in the wine country of Napa, a place she loved and where she had worked many of her summers. After the burial, our collective grief brought us together. Michelle's parents and mine were civil to one another. For a while, Michelle showed no anger when I suggested that we visit my parents. It struck me that it had taken the loss of my sister's life for Michelle to agree to spend time with my family. I wondered how many more lives would be destroyed or lost before my life with Michelle became truly normal.

twenty-eight

"Being with your dad at your sister's funeral made me think about what a hypocrite he is," said Michelle on an otherwise relaxed evening over dinner.

"Why do you say that?" I asked.

"He claims to be such a Christian. At Rachel's funeral he made that speech about love, and how Rachel was pure love. He said that she never judged anybody and treated everybody with kindness. He quoted the song that said, 'They will know we are Christians by our love.' Nobody would know that he was a Christian using that logic. You see the way he despises me. The way he makes me feel so useless and insignificant. Where is the love there?"

I wasn't sure how to respond to her charge. I knew that it was not so much that my father despised her as much as that he felt that my being with her had put an abrupt halt to my career and personal growth. Because of this, he saw her as playing a very significant role in my life while at the same time being a person of little consequence to him. He was angry with me for having made the choice that I did, but by disregarding Michelle's existence he had made an enemy who would not easily go away. He would have to deal with her whether he liked to or not. Further, I had told my father that he would have to come to terms with the fact that Michelle was indeed my wife, that his disrespecting her was doing equally so of me.

"And do you want to know what else I think about hypocrisy?" she asked further.

"What's that?" I asked.

"I think that everybody is a hypocrite. They all go about pretending that they are better than everybody else. You know me. I say exactly what I mean. Sometimes it's not that pleasant, but it's always true. I don't mince my words. I spit them out with a vengeance. People can't take that. And maybe I am a hypocrite sometimes, but you know what? I accept that. I know that there are contradictions in the way that I act and the things that I say. The worst hypocrisy is not to recognize that you are a hypocrite."

"You're right, I guess, but just saying that you are a hypocrite doesn't excuse bad behavior."

"I wasn't saying that it did," she countered, "but on the other hand, people know that I have borderline personality disorder. Your father knows it. You think that it is easy being me? I spend every day thinking whether I should continue trying, or kill myself instead. And it's because I can't take being who I am. It's because I can't stand that I make other people's lives so miserable. Do you think that your father could live by his own Christian values and show some understanding?"

Michelle's reflection had been clear and well reasoned. There had been little anger in her deliberation. I agreed with her, yet at the same time I understood that my father's opinion of her came not from a judgment of her character alone, but from his perceived sense that he had lost a son. In either case, the distinction was meaningless for Michelle. His attitude toward her was the same either way, and for this she hated him.

twenty-nine

EARLY MAY

I was assigned to spend the final two months of my internship in another surgery rotation. On the first day, the senior resident told me that the rotation would require my being on call overnight every third night, as well as doing rounds every Saturday and Sunday morning. Moreover, we had to be available to answer any questions about our postsurgery patients, even on our days off, in case the covering doctors had any questions. The requirement was to be within beeper range twenty-four hours per day. As beeper range was only ten miles, there was no way to live at Michelle's parents' home. I realized my luck. It was consistent with my plan to move Michelle farther away from her support systems.

Hesitantly, I told Michelle of the new schedule.

"You fucking miserable shit, you're disgusting!" she screamed. "Why can't you get a job where you aren't sticking your fingers up vaginas and up shitholes? Do you think that I'm attracted to that? If I had known what you do I would never have married you."

"Where are my keys?" I asked calmly.

"What, are you going to drive away again?"

Her parents, hearing the commotion, appeared at the bedroom door.

"You see what he is doing? He's trying to drive me crazy. He doesn't care."

"Where are my keys?"

"You want your fucking keys?" she growled. "You want your fucking keys?" she screamed again. "Well, here they are."

She had the keys hidden in her coat pocket. She took them out and ran at me. The ignition key was protruding from her fist as if she were holding a small knife. She brought it down toward my face, cutting into my eyelid. I jumped back, and my vision suddenly dimmed from the rush of blood that flowed from the cut. Michelle dropped the keys and ran, crying, to her room. I grabbed a sweatshirt from the floor to cover my eye, picked up the keys, and drove to my parents' house.

"Anthony, what happened? What did she do to you?" asked my mother.

"I don't know anymore, Mom. This whole thing is too big for me. I just can't do it anymore." The phone rang. "Don't tell her I'm here," I begged.

"It's one of your friends. It's a man," said my younger sister.

"Hello?"

"Hi. I knew you wouldn't answer, so I got my brother to call," said Michelle, always calculating. "I just wanted to talk to you. I'm so sorry; you really are the best thing that ever happened to me. I'm so scared that you will leave me that I lose control. Please just come back. I love you so much. I'm sorry."

Her rage quelled, I drove back and found her waiting, subdued, sitting with her parents in the living room. For a long

133

time no one said a meaningful word, and finally she came to sit with me.

"Promise me that you still love me," she pleaded.

I remembered the passion we had shared in that room more than a year ago, after the party at Tio's house, and I wondered where the freedom and fun had gone.

thirty

The moment after she stabbed me with the key, I realized I had been misguided in my belief that I could help her. She had always had a way of appealing to my sense that I could do something for her. She knew that and manipulated that. I too had manipulated her. I needed somebody to need me, although not as much as she did.

Emotionally I was tapped out. My sense of self and purpose had all but disappeared. Most disappointing was coming to terms with the fact that love, after all, could not in and of itself cure all the hurt in the world. Now the increasing certainty that I would leave Michelle, who was so rooted in her own self-destruction, was liberating. If she wanted to follow me to another residency, it would be knowing that this time there would be no turning back. There would be no familiarity to fall back on. If she decided to make the choice to follow me, it would be her last chance to make it with me.

The next morning I woke early, ready for the new rotation. I had bought an intern's guide-to-surgery handbook, but I couldn't find it that morning. I rushed out and stopped briefly at my parents' house.

"I know it seems that it's taken me a long time to figure it out, but I know that I have to leave Michelle, or at least I have to leave Miami and the security that it brings her. Unless there's a miracle, I doubt that she'll be able to make it away from her family.

"Dad, I know how you feel about Michelle, but I do deeply care about her. In those moments when we are having fun, it is the most fun that I have ever had. In those moments when she shows her caring side, she is the most caring person I know. It's unfair of you to think badly of her because of the choices that I have made. I made this mess, but I am going to get out of it."

My father tried hard to not show his joy, but immediately he offered me help. "I'll buy the ticket for you; I'll take care of everything," he said excitedly. My mother shook her head.

"Sometimes you can be so insensitive," she berated my father, then added, "Anthony, whatever you choose to do, just know that we love you. We will all get through this together."

I felt that I needed to take some time off before starting my residency. I needed to regain a sense of perspective and self. I decided to spend a year traveling through Europe, but first I needed to make some money. With my residency applications complete and being processed, I searched the medical journals and found a job posting looking for a part-time emergency room doctor in a London hospital. They were seeking assistance in dealing with psychiatric cases. I felt that the posting had been written for me. I called the contact number and was warmly told that as long as I could get all my work-visa paperwork approved and have my credentials verified, they would be glad to interview me.

I soon had an airplane ticket to Europe, a part-time job in

London, and a residency position in the works. The pieces were falling into place, but the biggest challenge lay ahead.

The idea of telling Michelle that I was ready to leave Miami terrified me. I had recurrent and increasingly paranoid thoughts that she could read my mind and its hidden deceit and that she would further discover the secret preparations I had planned. I was afraid of what she would do. She had used a knife to slash her girlfriend's car tires, for instance. Even a plain set of keys had been damaging. I was afraid to lie in bed with her. I was afraid to get into my car, fearing that she might have tampered with the breaks. I was afraid for my parents. I had the fantasy of simply packing my bags, going to the airport, and calling her from there: "Hi baby. I'm at the airport. I'm leaving. Bye!" Ultimately, it was clear that I simply had to tell her.

More than just wanting to leave Michelle, I wanted to leave the misery that my life had become. I had to take back control of my self, without allowing her to define my identity. In some fashion, Rachel's death had contributed to this decision. Her life, ended so young at twenty-two, had been more complete and full than my own. Further, as an even younger man, I had promised myself that no matter when I died, I would always want to have felt satisfied with my life up to that point. I had no satisfaction. Rachel had set her own course and followed it to the end. She had understood the need to control her own life, years before I understood it, but then again she had always been ahead of the boys.

Leaving Miami was not only just about what I wanted; I also held on to the belief that Michelle's life could be better than it was. I wanted for her to leave the family and friends that sheltered her from having to deal with her own madness. But this wish for her was independent of my decision to leave Miami. I would leave with or without her.

I still worried over the timing of telling her. There were eight weeks to go until the end of my internship. It was still far too early.

Michelle's parents and I had a relationship based on need. I needed them to take care of her when she was angry with me, and they needed me to take care of her when she was angry with them. It was an unstated understanding. I felt that they needed me more than I needed them. I could always leave Michelle, but she would always be their daughter. Because of this, they tried as best they could to make my life as comfortable as possible. Increasingly, I had become suspicious of their every act of support and kindness. I felt that they would do anything to keep me with Michelle. I had always been able to talk to both of her parents, but Michelle's mother called the shots in the family. I decided that before I told Michelle of my plan I would tell her parents. They had their own interests to care for. Together we would come up with a solution.

When I played out the scenarios in my head, I realized that I wasn't telling Michelle that I was leaving her. I was offering her a choice, even though I knew that it was a choice that would be very hard for her to make. It was a choice between deciding whether to stay with me on terms that were far less hers than mine, or to allow me to leave her. "People always end up leaving me," she had told me on so many occasions. I wanted her to have a choice in the matter, without it being unilateral. She had professed to me many times that no one had ever loved her as much as I had loved her. Perhaps the fear of losing such love and commitment would shock her into realizing that she had to break away from the toxic routines and supports that she so relied on. I had seen enough good in her that I felt if I could just cut out the bad part, I would have been happy with what was left. But I also knew that she was who she was because of her whole and that it was this complexity that had, in part, mystified and tantalized me.

I was disappointed that my love for her had not cured her and that I would likely end up leaving her because of her inability to change. In my naïveté I had been hurtful to her, building up her hope that this time would be different. And yet others had begun to see small positive changes in Michelle too. She had been able to hold down a job for four months, longer and more consistently than ever before. Also, the times of crises were fewer and further between. Although her attack with the key had come in the context of considering visiting my family, at least she had considered it. Instead of daily anger, the episodes of rage were reduced to a few times per week, and they didn't seem to last as long as before. Was it just that I was more used to her outbursts, or that I knew what to do to avoid them? Perhaps knowing that I was leaving put me into survival mode, getting through each day without attempting to challenge her.

Michelle's therapist asked her to invite me to their next session. I had been intrigued by the therapy for some time but had decided to stay out of it for fear that I would be seen as interfering. Michelle had been seeing the same therapist on and off for a year prior to her overdose. Since her discharge she had seen the therapist once or twice a month and then not at all while we were in Taos. She had reconnected on our return but had not seen her consistently.

I agreed to go with her, and we drove together to a beautifully landscaped private home not far from her parents' house. Her therapist was a large, well-dressed, motherly woman who readily hugged Michelle on seeing her. I wondered whether hugging rules applied to non-M.D.s. Michelle was involved in a type of problem-solving therapy with some attempts at insight interwoven through the therapy session. The therapist told me that Michelle had made a breakthrough in recognizing just how much despair I must have felt at not seeing my family, but that she feared that my connection to them would destroy my love for her.

All of this was good, but it had been at the expense of my own sanity and emotional resources. If she couldn't by now internalize that I loved her, I was too empty to try anymore.

thirty-one

I knew that I was just hours away from taking a profoundly significant action, one that would change the course of my life forever, and my whole being sensed it. There were times in the preceding weeks when I had imagined this day but was never brave enough to go through with it for fear that I would fail. That was my greatest fear.

The senior resident gave me the rest of the day off work. When I arrived home, Michelle was on an errand, so I used the opportunity to talk to her parents. I told them of my applications and interviews with the residency programs. I let them know about the part-time job in England, and that my father had paid for a ticket to Europe. They listened quietly. When I was done talking, Michelle's mother started to cry.

"This is going to kill her. Aren't you worried that she will kill herself? Why did you marry her? You remember how you met her. You promised her." It was my turn to be silent, and then we were all quiet.

"I'm not exactly leaving her. I just don't want to live this way anymore. I want my own house. I want Michelle to have to face hard choices without having easy solutions. I appreciate all that you've done, but this is not the life I want to live. This situation has not made her life any better, and it has certainly made mine worse."

"Anthony, she'll never make it," she protested.

"If she can't make it then we'll never make it together. I can't give up my dreams in order to spend the rest of my life taking care of her. Maybe I made a serious mistake; I loved her then and I love her now, but I can't give what I don't have left to give."

"You are leaving us to pick up the pieces."

"This is bigger than that. It is about my life too, not just hers. I'm dying inside. At the end of the day you'll have to pick up the pieces anyway. The only hope she has is if I'm strong enough to care for both of us. We have to get out of this hopeless spiral."

"We have to start preparing her. Don't tell her about your plans yet." They decided that they would let Michelle believe that they had lost faith in me, thereby distancing themselves from me. She would have them to turn to for support if she needed to.

After talking to them, I returned to our bedroom. I felt relaxed. More than relaxed, I felt an odd peace thinking about how my life had taken such a dramatic turn. With this peace came relief. Through the open closet door I saw one of my old belts hanging on a hook. I tried it on and felt disgusted that it didn't reach around my waist. I threw it back in the closet and then bent over to pick it up. I saw some torn papers lying on the floor. I picked them up and recognized my now shredded, long-lost surgery handbook. Michelle walked in. "Sorry," she laughed. "Your damned job just made me so mad."

During the long days of the surgery rotation and during the tension-filled moments that Michelle and I shared, I held on to the certainty of my leaving as if it were a life preserver. When we bickered or fought, I nearly blurted it out on each occasion. "You treat me like shit," I would say to her in my thoughts. "That is why I've had it. I went behind your back because I was terrified of what you'd do to me. I am leaving you because you don't let me breathe, because you don't share my dreams, because you are not my partner, because all you have ever cared about is yourself." But these were just thoughts that were driven by anger. I knew that she acted the way that she did because she was so afraid of being left alone or that she did not exist outside of me. She had no identity of her own, so she had hijacked mine, and now I had no sense of who I was. In order to be with me, she felt that she had to destroy anything that would get in the way of our being together, whether it was my love for my family or a simple textbook.

The days were passing slowly. In desperation I began to count down the hours, and then the minutes, and finally the seconds, notching them off in my diary, like a prisoner carving each day into the wall.

"My parents have become really down on you these last few days. They told me that they don't think you'll be able to take care of me. I told them to fuck themselves. God, sometimes I can't stand them, especially my father. He's such a wimp. I never told you, but once a friend of mine got me a gun. My father had grounded me because I came in late one night. Big fucking deal. He made it into such a big issue. He lost his fucking mind. I thought that he was going to beat the crap out of me. I locked my door and he kept banging on it to let him in. I sat on the floor facing the door, with the gun pointed at the door. I tell you, if he had forced his way in, I would have put a bullet in his head. He has no spine. He lets my mother walk all over him. He represents everything that I don't like in a man."

I wondered why she was telling me this story now. I feared that she still had the gun, but she told me that she had given it back to the friend. I wondered if her parents told her about my earlier conversation with them? Was she threatening me?

"Baby, you have taken better care of me than anybody ever did. I love you. I can't wait to get out of their house and find our own apartment." In that brief moment I felt affection for her that I had not felt in some time, but the offering was not enough to make me change my mind.

There were only five weeks to go. A humid Miami Sunday seemed about as right a time as any. I waited until after lunch to speak to her. We walked into the garden, away from the kitchen knives, scissors, and car keys. I could see her parents through the dining room window, pacing, looking back at us. She saw them too.

"What's going on?"

"I got a job in England."

"What are you talking about?"

"Also, I have been offered some interviews in Boston for residency."

"When did all this happen?" She looked at her parents suspiciously.

"I'm doing this for us," I said quickly, defensively. I told her of my applications, and my early-morning meetings with my father. I told her of the airplane ticket. I felt that I was back in my eighth-grade Catholic school confessional. She listened closely until I had stopped.

"You are such a liar. What you have done is worse than any slap in the face. It is worse than anything anybody has ever done to me. You sat there and planned the whole thing behind my back. Am I such a horrible person?"

She appeared suddenly calm. "You go on with your plans, but I swear you'll regret it. You know that I'll never trust you again."

Suddenly she became desperate again and pleadingly added, "Anthony, why now? I was doing so well. Why? Can't you see how I'm healing, how you're helping me? I promise, I'll see your parents whenever you want."

thirty-two

The following Friday I was assisting in an appendectomy when I got an urgent page to call home. The senior resident knew my situation. "Go ahead. I'll finish up here."

"Anthony . . ." It was Michelle's mother. "She's done it again. She's taken a whole bunch of pills. We had to admit her to the hospital. Please come over as soon as you can."

"I'll be there as soon as possible."

The resident gave me the day off and I rushed to the hospital. Michelle was sharing a semiprivate room with an older woman. I drew the separating curtain between them and sat on Michelle's bed. Memories of a year earlier flooded back. I held her hand.

"I lied," she said. "I just took a couple of Tylenol. I wanted you to come back. I'm not going to make it without you. You say that you're drained, but you were able to put all those application packages together. You're not as drained as you think."

"That was self-preservation," I told her.

"Just thinking about you going makes me miss you already. We haven't been able to talk about it because you spend all your time at the hospital. I haven't had a chance to be with you." A naughty smile spread across her face. "I want to show you something," she said, leading me to the bathroom, pillow in hand.

Her roommate lifted a tired head off her bed to look at us, then flopped back and closed her eyes. Michelle locked the door behind us, took my hand, and slipped it between her legs. "Can you feel how much I've missed you? I've been wet since my mother told me that you were coming to the hospital. I want you right now. I want to know that you still love me, and I want you to know that I still love you." She dropped her soft white cotton robe to the floor.

It had been months since we had been so uninhibited, but this time felt different to me. Early in the relationship, when we made love in the park or in a restaurant, it felt like it was part of the intensity that our relationship was built on and that the intensity would hold us together. Now I felt like a pretender, stealing a one-night stand with my own wife, knowing all the while that I was going to leave her and that she would not be able to make it with me outside of her safety net. For her, though, the mood of the moment was what was real. "I feel so whole when we make love. I know that we can make it together."

We dressed hastily and left the bathroom. I felt guilty that her roommate "knew," and I almost apologized. Her visitors looked at us suspiciously. The next day Michelle was discharged from the hospital.

I returned to work, and the hours spent in the operating rooms were long. Michelle spent an occasional evening with me in the apartment in Boca Raton, but we spent more time talking on the phone. Her mother called me frequently. Michelle seemed to be doing well, but her mother warned me that she was becoming more irritable. Michelle in turn told me that her mother was losing it.

One Saturday morning I had just finished rounds with the resident when my pager went off. "Doctor Walker, please call home. It's an emergency." The resident gave me a kind, sympathetic look.

"Take all the time you need," he said. I phoned home, expecting to speak to Michelle's mother, but Michelle herself answered.

"It's my mother. She took an overdose of pills this morning. They took her to the hospital. God, she is such a child!"

"We're done with rounds," said the resident. "Go."

On the drive home, I wondered if Michelle's mother was as sick as Michelle was. Maybe there was some genetic component. Maybe Michelle's mother had been so self-absorbed that she hadn't had the capacity to connect with Michelle and that had made Michelle so desperate for love. Maybe she wasn't so disturbed that she couldn't function, but this overdose seemed to me to be just as manipulative as anything that Michelle had ever done. I felt that she had done this to get back at me for threatening to leave Michelle. I wondered whether she thought that I would stay to take care of her, as I had taken care of Michelle just a year earlier.

It felt like I had married not one but two very disturbed and shattered women. "You are her guardian angel," her mother had told me. "Without you she would never have made it." I wasn't sure whether guardian angels were a big part of the Jewish faith, but these heavenly beings had been a cornerstone of my Catholic upbringing. Our angels would intercede for us to God and protect us from all evils, my parents had assured us. Maybe her mother using the term "guardian angel" had been a manipulation, appealing to my very early indoctrination. I saw manipulation in all of her actions, but I also understood why she did it. If she could not get somebody else to take care of her daughter, she would be the only one left to do it. Knowing her daughter, she had realized that she would never be able to do it alone.

Her mother looked tired and said that she was. When Michelle left the room to buy a box of chocolates, her mother sat up in bed. "It's so difficult to have her about the house without you being there. She takes so much. I can't do it on my own." The overdose had been minor, but she took the time in the hospital to rest.

"She is so manipulative," complained Michelle.

I couldn't wait to get out of the madness.

thirty-three

The final weeks passed calmly. Michelle seemed more withdrawn. "I don't know what I'm going to do. Just in case I don't make it with you, I've decided to start dating other men," she said without the hint of a threat. Previously she would use the threat of being with other men as a way to undermine my sense as a man, as a lover, and as a protector. Now it seemed like a realistic option. In a way I hoped that she could find somebody else. It would make my leaving easier.

Eventually my internship came to a merciful end. I had a week off before my trip to England, and we spent the time together. Each day Michelle appeared sadder. She cried frequently and begged me to change my mind, but her rage did not show. Unable to say good-bye, she told me that she was going to take a vacation in the Outer Banks with her parents rather than come to the airport.

With three days to go I had gone to my parents' house to pick up a suitcase for the trip. Michelle called me at my parents' home.

"I've decided that this whole thing is just not going to work out. I have to look forward to my future, and I don't see that being with you. You know that I can get anyone I want. I met this guy at work the other day. He came to the counter.

He's been coming to the counter a lot. He's got a lot of money. He asked me out. I have a date tonight."

"Fine."

"That's the way you want it? You're not going to stop me?"

"No, it's the way that you want it."

"If you don't want me to go, tell me now."

"It's your choice."

"I think I'll fuck him, maybe in the shower. He'll enjoy it. You know that."

"That's your choice too," I finished. She hung up. At seven that evening, she called me back.

"He's here. I just want you to keep the picture in your mind of him on top of me, inside me, kissing my breasts."

She hung up again. At eight she was back on the phone. She was calling from the restaurant.

"Babe, I'm having a terrible time. My stomach is hurting so much. I'm coming home now, please be there. You knew I would never do it. You have to know how much I'm going to miss you."

The next day she left, miserably, with her parents. "Call me every day. Promise me that you will."

thirty-four

I waited nervously at the airport, pacing back and forth in the departure lounge, waiting for the ticket counter to open. I waited nervously at the check-in line, and then waited nervously at the gate. I waited nervously in my seat by the window. I was certain that she would do something to stop me. Maybe she would come running down the ramp yelling and screaming, begging for a last chance, acknowledging that she had made a terrible mistake. I waited for the captain to announce that they had been ordered by the tower to delay the departure. The gate closed and we taxied back a few feet, then abruptly stopped.

"Good evening, ladies and gentlemen. We apologize for the abrupt stop but we have been ordered to stay in place . . ." I closed my eyes, ". . . as there is an emergency landing in the runway right in front of us. The delay will not be longer than twenty minutes."

I breathed a little but counted the seconds slowly. "One Mississippi, two Mississippi, three Mississippi . . ." Twenty long Mississippi minutes went by, and then we moved. I melted back into my seat and closed my eyes as the thrust propelled the plane further away from my fears.

After a brief layover in New York, I finally touched down in Boston, and then, with residency interviews complete, I looked out east across the Atlantic to Spain. I had not seen my grandfather in some time. I needed a complete break before my part-time job in England was to begin.

Madrid was only an eight-hour flight and yet a world away from everything I feared. Though the city air was polluted, it was the easiest I had breathed in a long time. The distance felt good. There was no threat of discovery, and I felt that I could do whatever I wanted to do. With every sip of sangria, the anxiety and tightness slowly washed away.

At moments I felt guilty for feeling good because it seemed that it was at Michelle's expense. It was precisely because she was not there that I could feel some peace. For what had felt to be an eternity, she had conditioned me not to feel any pleasure outside of her. Her fearsome tantrums had been intolerable in their wrath. Immediately I noticed that my sleep had improved. No longer did I worry that she might attack me in bed. My body felt more relaxed, my thoughts seemed slower and more focused. I felt that I could think about things without worrying about what Michelle would say or how she would react. But even with the distance from Miami, I felt her presence, and I jumped and startled when the phone rang or a car backfired.

The week in Spain refreshed me for the trip to England. The temporary job was in a North London hospital, covering for the psychiatry service in the emergency room. Landing in gray Heathrow, the clouds seemed not so menacing and the air was the freshest yet.

thirty-five

After three weeks apart, already I was beginning to forget the intensity of Michelle's rage, but the memory of her affection remained crisp, and for that I missed her.

Michelle and I had agreed to talk on a weekly basis when the daily schedule of phone calls had become too complicated to coordinate. One afternoon, after a quenching pint in a pub in the Archway, I made my scheduled call. She sounded upbeat.

"Sweetie, God how I miss you. It's taken me all this time to see just how good you are to me. I feel so empty without you. I realize that I can't go back to being without you. Everything has changed. I've treated you so badly. I've decided that I am going to do it. We are going to make our life together. I'm coming over to London next week."

That evening, the house of emotional cards collapsed. I felt nervous, defeated, and uncertain. I missed her, but I didn't know what I was going to do because I no longer believed that my love alone would heal her. I had promised her, though, that as long as she was willing to try to make the relationship work outside of Miami, I too would try to make it work. If she was going to take the brave step of moving away from all that was familiar and certain to her, I felt that I could not abandon her.

But what if she couldn't make it? We would be stuck in London with no one to turn to. Never had I felt so weak.

During the week waiting for her, I resolved to be strong, to not allow her to damage the small gains in self-confidence that I had made in the short time we had been apart, to not allow myself to give in to her rage. I had started to exercise and eat better, and in three weeks I had lost 5 pounds, dropping to 215. I increased the intensity of my running, knowing it would help.

Michelle kept her promise to come, and I picked her up at Heathrow. The sight of her familiar smile reminded me of all the joy we had shared. Suddenly I wondered whether my life with her had been as unpredictable and threatening as I remembered it to be. I realized how much I had missed her and that her unpredictability and spontaneity were things that had been attractive in the beginning. Why did I fear them now? Her face showed none of the torment and doubt that ravaged her mind. I waved at her and she started to cry, which made me cry. We rode a Black Cab back to the apartment and made tea. It all seemed so normal. I wondered if the separation had made a significant impact on her. I prayed that the apparent change would be real.

The eternity of our first few days back together was made all the longer by an unspoken yet mutually agreed upon gentility. Neither of us dared breathe lest we destroy the remnants of a once powerful, now fragile love. Yet love it still was, and so we held hands down Drury Lane on our way to see *Cats*. During the day, while I was at the hospital, she would rearrange the furniture in the apartment or paint flowers on canvas to add to the barren walls. We did not fight with the destructive passion that our days in Florida had seen, yet we made love with that same passion, for in that love there was no hurt. But the work that we needed to accomplish as a couple lay cemented in the past with all its pain, and although neither of us wanted to touch the unspeakable, it was with us throughout.

Three days after Michelle's arrival, we were invited for dinner at the apartment of an old friend who had been slumming around England for the better part of a year. We drank a little too much wine and decided to walk back home rather than risk the perils of the underground Tube.

"I see you had a good time tonight," said Michelle.

"I had fun. Didn't you?"

"Nothing's changed, it seems. You still need other people to make you happy. Is that what you've been doing all this time, having fun without me? What, I'm not good enough for you? You have to be with someone else to enjoy yourself?"

Immediately I realized that my hope that she had fundamentally changed was delusional. I recognized the futility of our relationship. This realization struck me with the same certainty and clarity that I had experienced when I first fell in love with her in the hospital. I was overwhelmed with sadness. The relationship was dead. I had been in love with the dream of sharing the intensity I felt for life with a beautiful, creative, fast-thinking, intense woman, but the morning had come and there was no time left for dreaming.

I am sure that I had always known that Michelle would never stay, even though for the briefest of hours I had hoped that perhaps she might. The change would be too hard. She needed far more support and familiarity. Despite her own unpredictability, she needed predictability more than anyone I knew.

Once again a gentility returned, but this time it was the awkward civility of two people going through the motions of being together without purpose and knowing that all that might have been is lost. We ate at restaurants or pubs in the evening, after I returned from work, and spent long, silent hours in movie theaters.

We did not sail the Thames because the water was "too stinky and dirty," she had said, but we did walk along its banks on our way to the National Gallery to see an exhibition of Impressionist art. Here, she was in her element. "The Impressionist reminds us that our experience of life is not universal, and that what we take from each encounter is never clear. It is the sense of the event that stays with us, emotionally and not visually."

Michelle seemed to lose herself in painting after painting. "There's a Degas," she said joyfully. "Do you know what he said? He said: 'A painting requires a little mystery, some vagueness, some fantasy. When you always make your meaning perfectly plain, you end up boring people.'"

Michelle had never bored me, but our time together was over, and four weeks after her arrival in London, she returned safely to Miami. She promised that she would come with me to Boston, but apart from one other occasion, that was the last time I saw Michelle. After she left, both written correspondence and phone calls between us dwindled.

When I found out that Boston University had accepted me into their psychiatry residency, I telephoned Michelle to let her know.

"You need to know that I met a guy. He's fifty but he owns a Rolls-Royce. He doesn't need to work so he can spend all his time with me. I don't love him, not like I loved you, but do you know what? Love is crap. It comes and it goes. I need someone who will take care of me."

Her words stung as I replaced the receiver. The sense of failure would take a long time to deal with. I wondered about my own judgment. How could I ever be a good psychiatrist?

I spent a year in London working, smoking, drinking, meeting new people, trying to forget my past year, and occasionally isolating myself, but at least I was free to wallow in my own sorrow. I couldn't blame my misery on Michelle's daily shifts in mood any longer.

thirty-six

JUNE 1987
BOSTON, MASSACHUSETTS

I arrived in Boston a year after leaving Miami, with two suit-cases and the money I had made in England. In three weeks the residency would start, and I was glad to have the free time to settle in. I rented a completely unfurnished apartment in the South End and ordered a mattress.

"We'll deliver next Friday between nine and one," promised the salesman. The apartment stood completely empty except for the refrigerator and the oven. I needed a bed before then, so I went on a shopping expedition and discovered an army surplus store where I found a canvas stretcher that would do until the mattress arrived. Next, I bought some towels, which would double as curtains until I could get those sorted out.

Boston in the summer was sticky. Walking through the city laden with packages was an unpleasant, sweaty expedition. I carried the stretcher on my back and found a general store where I bought a spoon, knife, and fork, a pot, a bowl, and some canned foods. After a long walk back to the apartment, I took a tepid shower and set up the stretcher.

I realized that I had nothing else to do. My mother had

once warned me, "Only boring people get bored." I had never thought of myself as boring, but at that moment I didn't seem to have the energy to do anything.

That night I heated up some noodles, but they didn't appeal. I tried to read a book but couldn't concentrate. I lay on the stretcher and realized just how lonely I was. After more than two years of never being alone—first being glued to Michelle, and then with all the acquaintances I had made in London—I felt that I needed human contact like a drug addict needs his drug. Ironically, my neighbor was a fairly successful prostitute, though I wondered if she felt any less lonely. Her professional endeavors added to my already intolerable insomnia. I lay awake, unable to settle on the uncomfortable canvas. At three in the morning my thoughts were filled with doubt and misery—doubt about my judgment and misery at the sense of having failed. I considered returning to Miami and maybe to Michelle, but I reminded myself of how much I had to lose. Finally, the thought that I could surely never feel this low again brought some relief, and I fell asleep.

When I awoke the next morning I had a new sense of purpose. I needed to succeed. I wanted to do so on my own, even though I felt exhausted after my year with Michelle and my year of isolation in London. I could barely wait for the residency to begin, and when it did, I worked harder than I had ever worked. Slowly the tide of depression began to turn. I had started to smoke but soon stopped. I ate healthier and ran a mile every day. I tested the waters of new friendships, quickly withdrawing at the mere hint of neediness.

Over time, Boston became a friendlier city. One afternoon,

after a visit to the Museum of Science, I took the Green Line inbound train. At Kenmore the crowd packed in after another Red Sox loss. The game-goers were making their trip on the B-train toward Boston College. In the crammed and hot subway car, I was grateful for having a seat. I was on my way to Brighton, to look at an advertised apartment. I had to move away from the South End apartment, which had been dirty and noisy and lonely when I moved in and had rapidly come to personify the aspects of my life that I was trying to exorcise. An elderly Dominican woman struggled up the stairs of the subway car. "*Se quiere sentar,*" I offered her my seat. "*Usted es muy amable,*" she accepted kindly. We spoke for a minute and then I was pushed back by a new infusion of westward travelers. I felt a tap on my shoulder, and turned to face a thin, attractive woman, perhaps in her early thirties.

"You speak Castilian Spanish," she noted.

"I do," I said self-consciously.

"I lived in Seville for two years. I love Spain. Where did you learn to speak it?"

"My mother is Spanish. I lived in Spain, and I visit my grandfather in Madrid."

"Are you new in town?" she asked.

"Yes, just starting my residency at BU."

We continued in this way until we reached Boston College.

"Well listen, I get off here," she said. "I am going to a theater presentation of African dance tomorrow evening. You said you lived in Kenya, didn't you? I have an extra ticket. Here's my number. Call me if you like."

She seemed nice enough, and engaging, but to so readily

161

invite a stranger on such a trip . . . What were her motives? Was she crazy? Did I dare call her? I had no judgment left. I had become pathetically incapable of making a date with a woman without anxiety overwhelming me. All this worry, and I hadn't even been on the date yet. Eventually I did go and enjoyed the dance, though not enough to make a second date. I wasn't ready for that yet.

I was mistrustful of kindness, especially from single women, confusing it for manipulation. I would go on dates but would not follow up for fear that there would be too much intimacy. I buried myself in my work, glad for the hundred-hour workweeks. Although I was exercising somewhat, I was not losing much weight. In part this was due to my overindulgence at the frequent drug-representative lunches, with particular attention given to the donuts. A year of hard work, though, made the year fly by. I began to laugh at myself, to trust my feelings and judgment. I was better able to relax, to drink wine for its own pleasure rather than to escape.

One evening, soon after I had moved into the new apartment in Brighton in late 1987, Michelle surprised me with a phone call. I wondered how she had gotten a hold of my number. She told me that my father had given it to her. "I told him that I wanted to talk to you about a divorce. He gave me your number in a heartbeat."

"How are you doing?" I felt strangely comforted by her voice.

"I was thinking of coming out to Boston to visit you. Just for two weeks. I promise. I feel that I treated you so badly during the time we were together. I just want to say that I'm sorry. I want to be your friend. I don't have to stay with you. You could find me a hotel room."

I wanted to believe that she had changed. I wanted this for me, but I wanted it for her even more. I still felt affection and cared for her, but I knew that my wish for her to be better could not make it so.

"Sorry, Michelle, we've been through too much for a visit to be good for either of us. It's so easy to forget all the stuff that didn't work out. We remember the good times because they brought us such joy. The other stuff drove us apart. There is still a lot of hurt that lies between us."

She was silent for a minute.

"I'll speak to you soon."

We spoke twice more by phone and then the phone calls ended.

As the workload became more manageable, I picked up my exercise efforts and ate fewer donuts. Within months, I was down to 180 pounds. In April of 1988 the Boston Marathon ran past my apartment down Commonwealth Avenue, just before turning off at Cleveland Circle. I was determined to qualify for the race and to use the tough qualification standard as a measure gauge of my own healing. A year later I was down to 170 pounds and ran the St. Louis Marathon in 3 hours 10 minutes, thereby qualifying for Boston. I was fitter and more determined to be in control of my life than I had ever been.

The issue of my marriage to Michelle remained. I was not with her and could not remain married to her. I was beginning to feel whole again. I needed to complete my break from her. I called my father and asked him to help me find a divorce lawyer. My father arranged it quickly, and two years after leaving Miami, I flew back home for a visit.

The day after I landed I had to present myself in court. I wondered whether Michelle would appear. I worried that she would contest the divorce. I turned each time someone entered the courtroom to see if it was her, but she did not show up, and as quick as our wedding ceremony had been, so were the divorce proceedings. Both had lasted five minutes.

POSTSCRIPT

JUNE 1988

On my first day of legal freedom, I took my mother to Coconut Grove for lunch at her favorite Indian restaurant. The trees adorning the sidewalks were greener than I had ever noticed them to be, and the air appeared to glow in the bright sun. My mother told a joke, the only one she ever remembers, and I smiled at her pleasure in telling it without reminding her that I had heard it a hundred times before. Walking along Grand Avenue, we were startled by the sound of screeching tires behind us. It was Michelle. She peered out of the driver's window, then smiled. Her smile had not changed.

"My God, look who's back! Where are you going? I knew you were in town but I thought you'd head right out. What are the chances?"

"Hi! We're headed for some tandoori chicken," I told her.

"Jump in, I'll give you a ride."

My mother hesitated for a second, then agreed. We arrived at the restaurant a few minutes later, and I sent my mother off. "Michelle and I have some unfinished business, Mom."

"Okay. I'll meet you inside."

"They still want to protect you from me," said Michelle, smiling but without malice. "I don't know how you ever put up with me. I treated you so badly."

She looked beautiful and relaxed. A part of me wanted to reach out and hug her and thank her, and tell her not to feel so bad, that our relationship had changed me forever and for the better, and that I hoped she was less tormented than when we were together. I wanted to tell her that I was sorry for not having been able to keep to my promise. I wanted to tell her that she looked lovely and seemed self-assured. I didn't tell her any of these things for fear they would be a tease and give her some false hope that we could be together again. Instead I said, "I treated you badly too. I promised you something I could not do. To stay with you forever."

"You and all the other men I've ever known," she said wistfully. "Hey, why don't we go out for dinner tonight, just for old time's sake? I'm sure you're going back to Boston soon. A meal, a drink, and then home. I promise. Okay, maybe sex too, but we're divorced, so there is no commitment."

She laughed. "Hey, I'm just kidding about the sex," she said, catching my confusion.

I looked at her and smiled. I remembered the day I met her, and how, even with the tubes and the intravenous lines, she had seduced me. I thought about how quickly I had fallen for her. I wondered briefly if a dinner would be so dangerous; but then the memory of the rest of the relationship returned.

"I'm glad you stopped. We hadn't had a chance to say good-bye. I don't think that dinner would be a good idea, though."

"Okay, well, think about it. Here's my number. Call me if you want."

She leaned across and kissed my cheek. I got out of the car. She smiled at me a final time and waved through a partially open window as she drove off. That was the last time I ever saw or heard from her.

As I stood there on the sidewalk, watching her disappear into the hazy heat of the Miami afternoon, an ambulance with its sirens screaming rushed by in response to some unknown emergency. The door to the restaurant burst open and my mother came running out.

"Mom, where are you going?" I shouted after her. She turned in disbelief.

"I heard the ambulance and I thought that she had done something to you. What took you so long?"

"We shared some incredibly intense times, Mom. It was time to say good-bye."

And with our good-byes said, the dance was over.

A FINAL NOTE

As a psychiatrist I have had many opportunities to work with sufferers of borderline personality disorder. During these interactions I have seen and heard things that reminded me of my relationship with Michelle and her family. Many old memories, and some anxieties, have been rekindled. With these patients I share a sense of deep emotion. I do not feel their sense of desperation and numbness, but I do understand how terrible their existence can be. My relationship with Michelle strengthened my understanding of others' suffering, and this has made me a better therapist.

My relationship with Michelle further taught me a lot about the way I think. It taught me to be more curious about myself, about my thoughts and feelings and motivations, especially when I work with borderlines. I feel that I understand borderline personality disorder in my bones. I also know how tremendously draining their illness can be for those who love them.

It is true that the life of the person suffering from borderline personality disorder, or BPD, is dictated and directed by the disorder. It is also true that to some extent the lives of those

168

sharing the sufferer's life are dictated and directed by BPD. It is a life of extremes: of anger and love, of sadness and joy, of hope and despair, and sometimes even of life and death. When behavior is driven by desperation, it can be easy to forget that the behavior is not a choice. It is much easier to be frustrated and angry, and to blame the sufferer.

Even though Michelle's presentation was fairly typical for someone with a severe form of the condition, on the whole, many of the people with BPD have fewer severe symptoms and may be able to function fairly well, including sustaining longer-term relationships and maintaining full employment. Certainly if 2 percent of the general population have the condition—that is, 120 million people on the planet!—99 percent of those have not been hospitalized. Many people have five or fewer symptoms. Some exhibit only one or two.

Although statistics show that between 1 and 2 percent of the general population suffer from this debilitating condition, in the adolescent residential setting where I work more than 50 percent of the teenage girls have histories of severe trauma and show many of the traits of BPD. The work is incredibly taxing but infinitely rewarding, as the young girls heal using the Linehan-developed dialectical behavioral therapy (DBT) model (see Appendix Three). If only it had been available in the early 1980s.

Treatment does require love, but more than love, compassion. The love that is needed is not a romantic love but a desire to care. It is easy to confuse the two because of the borderline sufferer's seductive neediness. It is a neediness that appeals to our desire to help. The error is to love without limits or consistency. The error is to be alone in caring for the sufferer. The error is to believe that love alone will cure.

169

Hope lies in time. Healing comes when the borderline patient eventually internalizes both a trust in others and a stable sense of self. These are developmental processes that take time to mature. The change can come, although slowly, in the care of someone who's compassionate and patient.

Living with anybody who suffers from a chronic illness can be emotionally taxing. Moreover, living with someone who has a chronic mental illness means at times having to accept erratic behavior, unpredictability, and loss of autonomy. No amount of intellectualization and rationalization about the illness can ever truly remove the sometimes ruinous effects on the relationship. It is frequently not the case, however, that the effects of a personality disorder are so destructive to a relationship, and as such I hope that my story will be seen more as a case study in such a relationship than as a cautionary tale.

APPENDIX ONE

THE TERM "BORDERLINE"

The term *borderline* is a historical term that many people argue should be changed. These patients were first described in the 1940s by psychoanalysts who theorized that this is a form of pathology lying on the border between psychosis and neurosis. Some clinicians see it as the border between sanity and insanity. Nevertheless, the term is confusing and further has increasingly and unfortunately been used as a pejorative for difficult patients, in particular difficult female patients. In my opinion, a far better term would be *self-destructive personality disorder*, which would be the psychological equivalent of an autoimmune disorder. Others have proposed *emotionally dysregulated personality disorder*.

Sadly, it is common—and wrong—to call any woman who is seen as manipulative, especially one who has emotional problems, a "borderline." We have to be careful so as not to misuse the diagnosis. Also, at the end of the day, we all manipulate at some level, and manipulation alone is certainly not enough to make a BPD diagnosis.

DIAGNOSTIC CRITERIA FOR 301.83
BORDERLINE PERSONALITY DISORDER

(Reprinted with permission from the Diagnostic and Statistical Manual of Mental Disorders, *Fourth Edition © 2000 by the American Psychiatric Association.)*

A pervasive pattern of instability of interpersonal relationships, self-image, and affects, and marked impulsivity beginning by early adulthood and present in a variety of contexts, as indicated by five (or more) of the following:

1. Frantic efforts to avoid real or imagined abandonment. Note: Do not include suicidal or self-mutilating behavior covered in Criterion 5.
2. A pattern of unstable and intense interpersonal relationships characterized by alternating between extremes of idealization and devaluation.
3. Identity disturbance: markedly and persistently unstable self-image or sense of self.
4. Impulsivity in at least two areas that are potentially self-damaging (e.g., spending, sex, substance abuse, reckless driving, binge eating). Note: Do not include suicidal or self-mutilating behavior covered in Criterion 5.
5. Recurrent suicidal behavior, gestures, or threats, or self-mutilating behavior.
6. Affective instability due to a marked reactivity of mood (e.g., intense episodic dysphoria, irritability, or anxiety usually lasting a few hours and only rarely more than a few days).
7. Chronic feelings of emptiness.

8. Inappropriate, intense anger or difficulty controlling anger (e.g., frequent displays of temper, constant anger, recurrent physical fights).

9. Transient, stress-related paranoid ideation or severe dissociative symptoms.

Familial Pattern

Borderline Personality Disorder is about five times more common among first-degree biological relatives of those with the disorder than in the general population. There is also an increased familial risk for Substance-Related Disorders, Antisocial Personality Disorder, and Mood Disorders.

Specific Culture, Age, and Gender Features

The pattern of behavior seen in Borderline Personality Disorder has been identified in many settings around the world. Adolescents and young adults with identity problems (especially when accompanied by substance use) may transiently display behaviors that misleadingly give the impression of Borderline Personality Disorder. Such situations are characterized by emotional instability, "existential" dilemmas, uncertainty, anxiety-provoking choices, conflicts about sexual orientation, and competing social pressures to decide on careers. Borderline Personality Disorder is diagnosed predominantly (about 75%) in females.

Prevalence

The prevalence of Borderline Personality Disorder is estimated to be about 2% of the general population, about 10% among individuals seen in outpatient mental health clinics, and about 20% among psychiatric inpatients. It ranges from 30% to 60% among clinical populations with Personality Disorders.

Course

There is considerable variability in the course of Borderline Personality Disorder. The most common pattern is one of chronic instability in early adulthood, with episodes of serious affective and impulsive dyscontrol and high levels of use of health and mental health resources. The impairment from the disorder and the risk of suicide are greatest in the young-adult years and gradually wane with advancing age. . . . During their 30s and 40s, the majority of individuals with this disorder attain greater stability in their relationships and vocational functioning.

APPENDIX TWO

WHAT CAUSES BORDERLINE PERSONALITY DISORDER?

There are many important and varying theories on this matter, although almost all researchers agree that BPD results from a combination of biology and environment. Here I present the biosocial theories of (arguably) the three leading researchers and thinkers in this field.

John Gunderson, M.D.
Although Gunderson has not articulated a definitive etiology on the disorder, he states that it is evident that environmental events have a great influence on gene expression, and that psychotherapies can influence neural capacities in the way that medications do. He believes that it is possible that early abuse or other traumatic experiences lead to neuropsychological difficulties in processing information and in memory. He points to interesting studies examining the neurobiological effects of early separation, some of which have shown, at least in monkeys, a clinical picture similar to that of abandonment depression. It can be expected that the impact of failed attachment will be detectable in brain imaging or neuropsychological mea-

sures that may become markers of BPD. He feels that having a better map of where and how messages are processed in the brain can assist teasing apart the competing theories of etiology. This work of mapping is only just beginning.

Marsha Linehan, Ph.D.

Linehan's main theory is that borderline individuals have difficulty regulating several, if not all, emotions. This is seen as a joint outcome of biological disposition, environmental context, and the transaction between the two during development. Linehan theorizes that borderlines are born with a biological tendency to react more intensely to lower levels of stress than others and to take longer to recover. In addition, they commonly are raised in environments in which their beliefs about themselves and their experiences are continually devalued and invalidated. These factors combine to create adults who are uncertain of the truth of their own feelings and who therefore tend to respond erratically and inappropriately—to overreact or underreact—to private experiences such as beliefs, thoughts, feelings, and sensations.

Linehan also is responsible for developing the dialectical behavioral therapy, or DBT, which is discussed in detail in Appendix Three.

Otto Kernberg, M.D.

Kernberg has suggested that patients with BPD internalize early pathological object relations. The use of primitive defense mechanisms, which healthier individuals outgrow during normal development, maintains these relations. Kernberg hypothesizes that in the early stages of development, the infant experiences the maternal figure in two contradictory ways. The first is the good mother who provides for, loves, and stays close. The second is the hateful, depriving mother who unpredictably punishes and abandons the child.

Kernberg believes that borderlines are distinguished from neurotics by the presence of "primitive defenses." Chief among these is splitting, in which a person or thing is seen as all good or all bad. Note that something which is all good one day can be all bad the next, which is related to another symptom: Borderlines have problems with object constancy in people; that is, they read each action of the people in their lives as if there were no prior context. They don't have a sense of continuity and consistency about people and things in their lives. They have a hard time experiencing an absent loved one as a loving presence in their minds. They also have difficulty seeing all of the actions taken by a person over a period of time as part of an integrated whole and tend instead to analyze individual actions in an attempt to divine their individual meanings. People are defined by how they last interacted with the borderline.

Other Important Findings
Larry Siever, M.D., writing in the *Journal of the California Alliance for the Mentally Ill* (1997), made the case for a biological basis to BPD. First he points out that BPD patients "tend to show greater responses to pharmacologic agents that may induce affective changes" than do patients with other personality disorders or a control group. "This dysphoric response," he adds, "parallels that seen in depressed patients, . . . suggesting that the cholinergic system may play a role in mediating the dysphoric affects" of the borderline. Siever also cites evidence

that serotonin is involved—"reductions in serotonergic activity are associated with impulsive aggressive behavior," a hallmark of BPD—and that impulsivity and aggression "seem to be heritable."

Michael Stone, M.D., in his landmark outcomes study *The Fate of Borderline Patients* (1990), found that 38 percent of BPD sufferers had experienced early loss; 19 percent of females and 8 percent of males had been victims of parental incest; and 13 percent of all borderlines had experienced or witnessed parental brutality.

In another study of sixty-one male subjects with BPD versus sixty non-BPD subjects, Joel Paris, M.D., et al noted in the *Journal of Nervous and Mental Disease* (1994) that the BPD group had a significantly higher rate of childhood sexual abuse, more severe sexual abuse, a longer duration of physical abuse, and increased rates of early separation or loss. They concluded that trauma and problems with fathers are important factors in the development of BPD in males.

G. Waller (1994) found that childhood sexual abuse prior to age fourteen rather than later in life was associated with a diagnosis of BPD in 115 females with eating disorders. Similarly, Kenneth Silk, M.D., et al reported in the *American Journal of Psychiatry* (1995) a 76 percent rate of sexual abuse in a sample of thirty-seven BPD inpatients.

B. Runeson et al (1991) reported that BPD patients who committed suicide showed more early parental absence, substance abuse in the home, and lack of permanent residence than other patient groups who committed suicide in a sample of fifty-eight consecutive suicides of people between ages fifteen and twenty-nine in an urban community.

S. Berzirganian et al (1993) found in a prospective study of 776 adolescents that maternal inconsistency coupled with maternal overinvolvement predicted the emergence of BPD.

Finally, Terri Weaver, Ph.D, and Gretchen Clum, Ph.D., reported in the *Journal of Consulting and Clinical Psychology* (1993) that significantly more BPD patients reported sexual abuse than did non-BPD patients in a sample of seventeen and nineteen patients, respectively. They also found that BPD families were significantly more controlling than were non-BPD families and that this factor significantly predicted dimensional borderline score even after controlling for sexual abuse.

In Summary
What can we extract from all this research? Studies show that many individuals with BPD report a history of abuse, neglect, or separation as young children; up to 75 percent of BPD patients report having been sexually abused.

While the exact cause of BPD remains unknown, both environmental and genetic/biological factors appear to play a role.

APPENDIX THREE

HOW IS BORDERLINE PERSONALITY DISORDER TREATED?

There are two broad categories of treatment for BPD: psychotherapy and medication. A combination of psychotherapy and medication appears to provide the best results for treatment. Medications can be useful in reducing anxiety, depression, and disruptive impulses. The relief of such symptoms may help the individual deal with harmful patterns of thinking and interacting that disrupt daily activities.

Medications, however, do not correct ingrained character difficulties. Long-term outpatient psychotherapy and group therapy (if the individual is carefully matched to the group) can be helpful. Short-term hospitalization may be necessary during times of extreme stress, impulsive behavior, or substance abuse.

The treatment is often difficult and long term. This is because the ingrained maladaptive personality traits have developed over many years. Symptoms of the disorder are not easily changed and often interfere with therapy. Periods of improvement may alternate with periods of worsening. Fortunately, over time most individuals achieve a significant reduction in symptoms and improved functioning.

A major breakthrough in therapy is dialectical behavioral therapy, or DBT. This is a broad-based cognitive behavioral treatment pioneered for BPD by Dr. Marsha Linehan in 1991. DBT is based on the idea that psychosocial treatment of those with borderline personality disorder is as important in controlling the condition as traditional psychotherapy and pharmacotherapy are. DBT was the first psychotherapy shown through controlled clinical trials to be effective with this disorder.

Psychosocial skills training, one form of DBT that has been shown to be effective with borderlines, is a combination of individual psychotherapy and skills training. The basic theory is this: Some people, due to invalidating environments during upbringing and due to biological factors as yet unknown, react abnormally to emotional stimulation. Their level of arousal goes up much more quickly, peaks at a higher level, and takes more time to return to baseline than people without the condition. Because of the combination of biology and invalidation, these people don't have any methods for coping with these sudden, intense surges of emotion. DBT is a method for teaching skills that will help in this task.

Medication may be needed as part of outpatient treatment. Patients with marked mood swings sometimes benefit from two drugs ordinarily used to treat epilepsy, Depakote or Tegretol. Patients with severe depression or eating disorders may benefit from antidepressant medication. Small doses of the neuroleptic drugs typically used for schizophrenia sometimes help borderline patients in periods of severe stress. Benzodiazepine medication, such as Ativan, should be considered only with caution since they are dangerously habit forming and may lead to disinhibition of behavior.

If outpatient therapy is interrupted by repetitive suicide attempts, hospitalization is sometimes necessary. A thorough assessment may lead to the recommendation of a more specific individual therapy, adjunctive group or family therapy, referral to substance abuse treatment, or more intensive treatment in the form of hospitalization or a day-hospital program.

DO OTHER PSYCHIATRIC DISORDERS CO-OCCUR WITH BPD?

The answer is yes, and it is important to mention this under treatment. BPD may be accompanied by serious mood disorders such as depression and bipolar disorder, eating disorders, and significant substance (drug) abuse. About 50 percent of people with BPD experience episodes of serious depression. At these times, the "usual" depression becomes more intense and steady, and sleep and appetite disturbances may occur or worsen. These symptoms, and the other disorders mentioned above, may require specific treatment.

If a specific mood disorder is diagnosed, medication would be indicated, although care has to be taken that this medication is not used as a source of potential overdose. Specific treatment for eating disorders or substance abuse should be initiated.